The mind forgets,
but the heart always remembers,
that love does last.

by A.E.J.

WILL THE REAL WOMEN...

PLEASE STAND UP!!!

QUANTITY SALES

Knowledge Concepts books are available at special quantity discounts when purchased in bulk by corporations, organizations and special interest groups. Custom printing or excerpting can also be done to fit special needs. For details write: Knowledge Concepts Publishing Co., P.O. Box 973, Cedar Hill, Texas 75104-0973. Attn.: Special Sales Department.

INDIVIDUAL SALES

Are there any Knowledge Concepts books you want but cannot find in your local stores? If so, you can order them directly from us. You can get any Knowledge Concepts book in print. Simply include the books title and author (no cash can be accepted) for the full retail price plus $3.00 to cover shipping and handling. Mail to Knowledge Concepts Educational Systems, P.O. Box 973, Cedar Hill, Texas 75104-0973.

WILL THE REAL WOMEN PLEASE STAND UP

by Ella Patterson

"I've been looking for a book that told it like it really is. I've finally found that book in <u>Will The Real Women Please Stand Up</u>."

-Sonia Alleyne, Editor-in-Chief
Black Elegance Magazine

"I think that a book like this is needed for all women, I've enjoyed it."

-Diane Hendy, Editor-At-Large
Black Elegance Magazine

"A book that every women and man should have."

-Marva Houston, Flight Reservations

"In this book, Ella helps those of us who think we already know it all."

-Denise Hilliard,   Federal Officer

"No one should be without a copy of this book."

-Easy Street, Dallas Disc Jockey

"I finally found a book that I can learn from, I mean really learn from."

-Carmen Pagano, Radio Host

"This book will bring joy and sexual pleasure to your life."

-Janet White, Courier Service,

"Single women need this book because it's easy to get a man, but we need to know how to keep a man."

-Brenda Harper, Math Specialist

"This book shows sexuality from a fresh point of view."

-Carol Murray Sullivan, CEO-Bianca's
Deli

PREFACE

The last half century has seen many fundamental changes in the structure of society. Improved health habits have contributed to longer expectancy in women. Women live longer and enjoy their health consciousness more now than at any time in history.

Women play an important role in our society and assertiveness in many spheres; bringing creativity, values, attitudes and structure to their lives. The woman's movement, along with the sexual revolution, has given rise to sexual preference and sexual freedom. Based on female education, knowledge, sophistication and demand "to know", women want the freedom to do the picking and choosing of their sexual partners.

Women are no longer submissive to men when it concerns their bodies. Women are the ultimate decision makers with their sexual partners. Women are taking their bodies back. Men are seen as concerned contributors, but it is the woman who actually decides who she makes love to.

WILL THE REAL WOMEN PLEASE STAND UP is a compilation of female sensuality that women encounter throughout their sexuality. While accurate sensuality is not a cut-and-dried composition of facts, it is an account of fascinating secrets, solutions and games for contemporary women. In addition, this book presents women with choices, pleasures, entertainment and optimistic common sense on sexual freedoms. This book is for the "real women" who wish to give the fullest sensual, romantic and sexual satisfaction to their mates. It is also for the women who realize by doing so, she can give satisfaction to herself.

WILL THE REAL WOMEN PLEASE STAND UP is not just a sex manual. It is about complete sensuality. It describes basic hygiene and numerous ways to use this knowledge on sensuality to stimulate your mate. It does so without reducing wholesome sexual pleasures to a list of statistics and manual manipulations.

This book is filled with suggestions, games, and erotic techniques. But it should be remembered that these are only suggestions toward complete female sensuality and nothing more. If there are any that violate your personal sexual code of ethics, skip them and try others. It is your right to reject any of them as well as experience the pleasures of them. Some may be especially appealing to you and your mate. And as always, you may want to incorporate your own with these suggested. Enjoy yourself, but try not to create barriers that exclude you from further sensuous explorations. Patterns have been known to create boredom. Not all entries in this book are sexual, but all will help to validate and add something special to your relationship. This book is the starting point for your new found sexual happiness.

Happy Sexuality

ELLA PATTERSON

WILL THE REAL WOMEN...

PLEASE STAND UP!!!

Will The Real Women Please Stand Up, by Ella Patterson
Published by **Knowledge Concepts Publications**
P.O. Box 973
Cedar Hill, Texas 75104

Knowledge Concepts Educational Services,
P.O. Box 973, Cedar Hill, Texas 75104.
Library of Congress Cataloging in Publication Data
Ella Patterson, 1994
Will The Real Women Please Stand Up

ISBN: 1-884331-01-7

Library of Congress Card Catalog Number: 94-75061
Printed in the United States of America
Typography by Ella Patterson
Designed by Ella Patterson
Written by Ella Patterson
Edited by Lucille Ennix and Marvin Whaley
Cover and design by Ella Patterson
Graphic Illustrations by Larry Strader
1st Printing, January 1994 Library of Congress Cataloging in Publication Data
This book includes an index
Quotes obtained from *1000 Reasons To Think* by Ella Patterson
$14.95 Paperback

OVERVIEW

I interviewed women between the ages of 15 and 79. These women openly talked about sensuality and the sensitive side of their sexuality. I discovered many amazing things about many women throughout my research. All women have sexual secrets, motives, dreams, beliefs and desires. What classifies them as being real women is purely a matter of opinion.

I was informed by these women that the majority of women don't confer with one another with the intent to spread gossip. They merely talked to one another to learn so that they could experiment or try new things on their own partners. Many described ways to incorporate sensuous spice, add adventurous allure, bring teasing tantalization and become pleasingly provocative as they sensuously welcomed sexuality in relationships whether culturally accepted or not. They didn't allow society to determine their sexuality.

These women informed me of their need to achieve orgasms with or without intercourse; orgasms were a matter of priority for most of them. Women who experienced masturbation enjoyed it, and clitoral stimulation was a big issue with almost every one of them.

This book gives startling, informative and a true look at real women standing up for their rights to be strong, sensuous and sexy, without being weakened or threatened by ancient myths of sexuality.

Women gave me two main reasons for their candid responses and remarks. One, they wanted to be true to themselves, and two, they were simply REAL WOMEN.

ELLA PATTERSON

WILL THE REAL WOMEN...

PLEASE STAND UP!!!

™

KNOWLEDGE CONCEPTS EDUCATIONAL SYSTEMS

This one's for ...

All those women who have taught me that life goes on.

Prepare for life and live.
Prepare for old age and grow old.
Prepare for death and die.

ACKNOWLEDGMENTS

This book is a personal retrospection of the author. I attribute experiences gained during my research to many individuals. I am indebted to those friends who, over the past eight years, knowingly and unknowingly contributed to my data. This book speaks for itself. Select the parts that interest you and leave the parts that don't to those who choose to dig for a deeper understanding of the female sensuality. Everything is not for everyone, but I guarantee that there is information for every woman in this book.

While, WILL THE REAL WOMEN PLEASE STAND UP is not a clinical treatise, this information is derived from very intensive research. My gratitude goes to teachers, coaches, hair stylists, radio disc jockeys, college students, dentists, doctors, lawyers and preachers for their interest and undying support. Numerous others aided generously by encouraging me to forge ahead and seek my dream. Others helped by proofreading and by expressing their ideas. They gave me honest and open criticisms.

I owe my most spirited thanks to my husband Martin "Pig" Patterson Jr. for his ever-present inspiration and encouragement, as well as his dedication to my venture. To my children, Juanna, T'Juanna and Martin III, I give my eternal adoration. For many reasons, my warmest thanks and undying love to my best friend Robert Corley, and to my eternal friends Janet White and Marva Owens for helping me to put my thoughts onto paper. Special thanks to Argie Johnson, who taught me that love does last. And to my mom, Elizabeth Jones, who taught me that no matter what...life goes on, so you might as well enjoy it. And of course love and kisses to my oldest brother Herbert for his financial support and constant encouragement. I love you dearly.

I give thanks to God who in Jesus name, gave me the strength to do the research, and the ever-present courage to write this book along with the endurance to seek and find willing women that would openly talk to me about their sexuality. And God, please let Oprah Winfrey read my book too.

ELLA PATTERSON

WILL THE REAL WOMEN

PLEASE STAND UP!!!

Table of Contents

**You get what you expect,
whether conscious or unconscious.**

™

INTRODUCTION:

<u>WHY</u> <u>A</u> <u>BOOK</u> <u>LIKE</u> <u>THIS</u>

For many years, men and women have told me some of the most fascinating things about myself, that I'm very sensuous, sexy, beautiful, exciting and intelligent. I've had men to approach me with one of the oddest requests of all:
"Can I get to know you better?"
"Why?", I ask.
"Because you appear to be an interesting person !"
Many men have begged me to be their woman. Yet, you'd never guess by looking at me because on most occasions I'm friendly, but very conservative. I've received marriage proposals from men as old as seventy and as young as eighteen. These men are as diverse as college athletes to television and radio personalities.

I have excellent posture, beautiful hazel eyes, flawlessly smooth skin, long beautiful legs, small feet, full luscious lips, and a pulsating tongue to accompany my snappy vaginal muscles.
Depending on the mood, I wear short tight skirts, low cut blouses, skimpy dresses and I go comfortably without panties or hosiery. I'm intelligent, witty, and have a personality that is wholesome somewhere within my *bitch-like*

qualities.

Men and women come to me for advice and, out of curiosity, they want to know me. Through intelligence and observation, manipulation and concentration, you, too, can become a sensuous woman to the man of your choice.

Becoming a beautiful woman who men cater to is very difficult sometimes. We, as women must give pampering and affection to get our rewards of the same. It's been said that most men want a woman with:

~more than beauty
~more than brilliance
~more than a clean home
~more than being a mother for his children
~more than fine gifts
~more than a fashion conscious woman

He wants a multi-talented and sensuously mature woman. Sensuously mature women make men feel more loved and more cared for than they will ever be able to handle.

Women who cook, clean, speak well and are good mothers come a dime a dozen, but a sensuous woman, who can make her man feel like he's the world, will be worth the world to him. Any woman can open the doors of sensuality and sexual satisfaction if she opens up her mind and rids herself of the myths of "nice girls don't do that" thinking. To explore, discover and accomplish the how-to's of erotic pleasures that await you and your lover, began reading. Turning the page will open your eyes to why a book like this is needed and so important to all real women. Real women want to please their men in rich, rewarding and nurturing ways. The real woman must take a stand and finally discover her own sensuality and sexual capabilities by taking all the necessary steps to please her man. He will, in return, take care of her needs, wants and desires.

Chapter 1

™

BECOMING A REAL WOMAN

WHAT IT'S GOING TO TAKE

You're about to change your life. Inside this book you'll find everything you've ever needed to know about being a real woman, but were afraid to ask. It's all here for you: the most current sexual trends; money-saving ideas to please you and to satisfy your man; tricks of the trade that everyone will want to know. In this book you'll find the secrets of how successful women turn their men on. Your personal confidence level will rise to heights of complete positive acceptance, and you'll do the right things to be the total woman in business as well as in bed. Whoever said that business and pleasure don't mix was probably a dull fuck and was also handling sex and business in an inappropriate way. The idea of you being a real woman is only a thought away. It's time for women to do the right thing by enjoying love, life, sex and the pursuit of happiness in the bedroom without feeling shame or guilt. This book is for those who claim to be real women, and those who someday want to be.

This book will help you in so many wonderful, positive and rewarding ways when trying to:

~find men
~meet men
~seduce men
~go on a diet and keep the inspiration to stay on it
~attain fabulous breasts from those you already possess
~select the most sensuous lingerie without loosing the support you need
~wear sensuous shoes: from bedroom slippers to tennis shoes to high heels
~be the queen of his night and the lady of his wet dreams
~dress seductively without looking like a tramp
~kiss very sensuously and not tell
~get more of what you want from men
~have women at your feet and not be lesbian
~remain romantic in and out of bed
~sexually stimulate with every part of your sensuous body
~be sensuous and not be considered sleazy

I've been listening to women complain about what their men want, what their men aren't doing to satisfy them and how they want to turn their men on more. I've read every book on sex and relationships that's been printed for the past fifteen years and they all seem to say the same things. They say enough of what we want to hear, but not enough of what we really need to know. My book is concerned with what women of all colors want and need to know about complete female sensuality.

I am a wife/mother/friend/teacher/coach/author/business woman and now professional speaker extraordinaire. Through my many talents I've been able to learn from my opportunities. My years of good tips trials, and tribulations have made me an authority on sensuous street savvy and romance. There is an art to being a contemporary women of vision with sensuous attributes.

The ingredients to be this woman of vision with an adventurous spirit are the keys to unlocking the complexities of a REAL WOMAN. And only a woman can do that.

I was born and raised in East St. Louis, Illinois. In a short time, I learned the ropes of self-marketing, the magic of being a good listener, the value of true friendship, the ups and downs of media support, and the blessings that come with knowing how to pray. Since I'm of Irish decent, I give luck plenty of credit also.

I've always been told to know the rules, but I've found out that not knowing all of the rules has many advantages. Whether I'm at work or at home, with friends or with lovers, from night life to day life, I follow my guidelines of sensuality. The way to a man's heart is through his woman and the way to a woman's heart is through her man. Each must have something unique to offer the other in a positive, beneficial, and exciting manner. After all, nothing is free, not even the love that you think you give so freely. I'll get more into lover's benefits later in this book.

The purpose of this book is to share my knowledge with you. My sincere objective is to bring to you the things that absolutely turn men on. I will give to you the things that women have told me about love, happiness, relationships, sex, and fulfillment in life. Being a sexy, interesting, romantic, open minded and confident woman in all situations is only partially the scope of this book. I'll show you how to have fun in life by taking your best attributes of being a woman and fusing them with strength, independence, self-esteem, intelligence, etiquette, and confidence. You'll be able to enjoy your sexiness as you confidently adore men and still feel beautiful as you are given love. You will begin to notice a difference in how you look, how you feel and how you think about yourself. Your personal effectiveness and how you communicate with others will improve. So become diligent and get ready to love the new you.

Bring knowledge to your mind.

TM

Chapter 2

GETTING PREPARED

Take your book <u>WILL THE REAL WOMEN PLEASE STAND UP,</u> and locate a quiet, comfortable and secluded place to read. Get your favorite drink; it doesn't necessarily have to have any alcohol content, just as long as it's your favorite. Find your favorite lounge wear, get comfortable and snuggle up until you feel cozy. Take the phone off the hook, and if you have to send the entire family to the movies for a few hours or so, do it.

As you began to read <u>WILL THE REAL WOMEN PLEASE STAND UP,</u> allow no distractions to interfere with the learning process. You are about to wake up to a whole new, exciting, motivated, vibrant and fulfilling mental awareness. We'll name this area your Sensuous Zone. Some of the discoveries in this book will allow you to use the sensuous thinking of your brain. Once these sensuous centers are awakened, many doors will be opened, unexpected doors. When these doors began to open and create this wonderful sensitivity, so will the possibilities of a more fulfilling existence.

PREPARING YOUR ENVIRONMENT

Your environment must include you. The mood should exemplify a pleasant and welcome invitation. It should be clean and it should represent your personal self. Your environment will include the people who are going to make love, so it should have an wholesome atmosphere. To make love in a bed with cracker crumbs or dirty linens is not healthy nor inviting. Give your lover a reason to be taken to your bed for other than sex. A clean and fresh environment is the first step toward a clean and healthy association. If your partner knows that you're clean, you hope he'll work to present a clean and healthy relationship as well.

Placing romantic scents and beautiful linens in your bedroom will send out pleasant signals to your special guest. Many women have found that a clean and fresh smelling living environment is a major asset.

Getting rid of all the dingy bed linens, those with holes, stained, torn or full of lint balls can make you feel more sensuous when slipping onto your bed. When washing your bed linens use fabric softener and a small amount of lingerie soaps to enhance the aroma as well as soften the texture. These additions to what you already have will add romance and sensuality. Aromatic candles create scents as well as special effects.

Chapter 3

FINDING HIM

WHERE TO MEET MEN

As a sensuous woman, you're not looking for just any man. You're looking for a certain type of man, a man who will turn you on physically, emotionally and intellectually. Be realistic about the mental image that you create of the ideal mate. While creating this perfect image, picture if you will, the type of man who will be attracted to you.

Be honest and give yourself a critical self-evaluation. In today's society it is considered more acceptable for a woman to go hunting for the man she wants. Men have always been entitled to pursue women who have attracted their attention. Even though some women prefer to be chased and seduced, there are situations that occur for many reasons that allow women to become more aggressive in their hunt. To keep from becoming overly aggressive, woman must manipulate her prey before he will completely appreciate how much she yearns for him.

Men have an extraordinary lack of self-confidence when it comes to meeting new woman. Most men who have inflated egos and believe that they are attractive to all women are still encountered. They usually act as either shy, tongue-tied, too macho, over boastful, or they lean over backwards to impress.

It takes a mature and confident gentleman to enjoy, without personal judgment, a direct approach from a mature and confident woman. A woman must first make up in her mind what she wants in a man as well as what she wants from a man. Some woman want regular meals in the finest restaurants, rides in the classiest cars, and fur coats of the highest quality. There are rich men with no looks who would be glad to provide these luxuries. There are also men with great looks who would be happy to equally provide these luxuries. My rule is to never criticize gold diggers because every living woman has a right to be happy whether financially or physically.

Today's society encourages give and take, and supply and demand, so a woman should give her man what he wants and then he'll let her take as much as she wants. She should supply her man with what he wants and then demand what she needs. A man loves the idea of having a sensuous, sensitive and beautiful woman on his arm and in his bed. I have found through research and observation he's usually willing to pay the price to get her too.

TM

Chapter 4

GETTING THE MAN YOU WANT

PROVEN TECHNIQUES

The best way to land a lover is to become fatally and irresistibly attractive to him. You're going to have to be warm, attentive, attractive, and you must carry a permanent glow on the inside and out.

Before you go any further you must know the answers to a few questions.
*Does the man of your dreams possess the qualities that you feel are satisfactory?
*Does he have generosity as well as integrity?

Men who aren't generally generous with their resources won't be generous with their love, affection and caring. Generosity depends on the man involved. Many men who are wealthy aren't necessarily generous. Some men are generous with their time, some are generous with their advice, and some are generous with their sex. The generosity that's being focused on here is SPIRIT.

Generosity is the time he makes for whenever and for whatever your needs. And for you to be just as generous to him is worth the giving. Knowing what you need as a woman is great, but knowing what you want in a man is fantastic. Be sure you know what qualities you seek in a man and then be just as sure the man you select possesses these qualities.

A woman can find ways to seek out the qualities that she wants in a man. Whatever that most important quality is, find it. Expect it and then demand it. Don't cheat yourself. Expect the best for yourself by expecting what you want as a woman. Expecting these qualities in the man who you've chosen is not being selfish, it's being sure of what you want in a man and that means not to settle for less. Your happy life starts with you, and as a woman, your happiness is your number one priority. Here are some proven techniques to help you get the man that you want:

1. BE ATTENTIVE TO HIM:

Have the ability to focus on a man with all of your attention. Become so genuinely engrossed in what he's saying that he's your only focus. Be able to look him right in the eye and give him your complete interest and concentration. Making him feel that he's the most brilliant man you've ever met is the key.

2. LEARN TO BE CONVERSANT:

Men like to talk about themselves. So you've got to be able to ask questions that will make him want to go on and on about himself. Winning questions consist of snoop questions. You might be bored with his likes and dislikes, but you've got to overcome your selfishness and focus in on what makes him tick. What makes him tick is you, being in awe about him. Don't think of it as being nosy either use good judgment on what you ask and practice the art of conversing. Start with something simple, like his business or his hobbies. What's his favorite vacation spot or his favorite food? Ask personal questions that aren't intimidating, like who's his favorite movie star, or what's his least favorite food. Even questions such as, do you still have your favorite childhood toy, can spark an interesting conversation with him.

Remember to look him straight in the eyes as you talk to him; this will bring out those things he always wanted to tell, but didn't think anyone wanted to hear. He'll love it and he'll love you even more for being interested enough to let him brag about himself.

3. DON'T BE AFRAID TO FLATTER HIM:

Self-esteem and inner strength aren't listed as finer qualities in men. Men may look stronger on the exterior, but their interiors are weaker than the most delicate women. Men need to be told that they are beautiful and that they are great in bed. Get in the habit of telling your man that you find him irresistible and gorgeous. Most women find it exhilarating and challenging to offer compliments to a man. For those men who need to be complimented or reassured, be especially attentive to them. Don't get caught up in flattering by telling lies. Compliments that are lies hurt people in the long run. They know when a lie is a lie on most occasions. Don't you?

4. BE AVAILABLE:

Playing hard to get has its virtues, but don't entertain this idea for too long a period unless there's a reason for it. Be available, supportive, and never play too hard to get. Saying no to a man too soon can be premature. A man generally wants to show a woman that he cares, so when he asks you to join him don't be so quick to say no. Don't let yourself hold you back. Learn new things by not joining the hard-to-get club. Men enjoy women who are available. Being available does not mean doing things that you don't like. It simply means learning new things with a man who you've chosen. Having the right attitude will display the character and principles that are needed to prove your own tastes and this alone will improve your self-esteem. You don't have to be a snob by constantly saying "no, or not this time". Sharing in his life in a positive and rewarding way will help him to miss you when you aren't around.

5. CONTINUE TO HAVE FUN:

Sometimes he won't be able to assist you or accommodate you and you'll be disappointed about it. Make your needs attractive to him by sharing the fun. By this I mean if you like to go to the movies and he'd rather stay at home and watch old reruns, compromise. Why don't you rent his favorite movie that you also like and without forcing him to go out to the movies, enjoy a romantic evening and top it with his favorite dessert...YOU. The compromise can be worth it if it becomes something the both of you can enjoy. Turn your fun into spicy enchantment. Keeping his needs in mind can be fun and in return he'll begin to focus in on your needs because you'll be the one in charge.

6. BE WHAT HE LIKES IN A WOMAN:

Being straightforward with your man and asking him what he likes can open many doors of pleasures between the two of you. If he knows that you like him and you treat him better than any other woman, he'll like you more. If a man knows that a woman desires him, she becomes more desirable to him. Never be scared to show him that you desire him. Let him know that you desire his warmth and affection. Touch him as often as you possibly can; stroke his sideburns. And if he doesn't have any, stroke his face. Men will respond to these gestures in a positive way. They love this kind of contact. Extending warmth and demonstrative touching doesn't have to be sexual. Any woman or man of quality knows the difference between warmth and sexual aggression. Men adore human touch because it shows the affection that they so badly miss and need. If a woman is self confident, warm and caring, men will be attracted to her. Men also cherish a woman with something to give and who is comfortable with herself. Remember to get what you want, you sometimes have to ask for it.

7. BE FAMILIAR WITH LIFE'S PLEASURES:

Convey a combination of glamour, happiness and directness. Being blunt and feminine at the same time is found to be provocative to men. Don't be afraid to speak what's on your mind to the man you're interested in. Clear speaking and confident talking women are sexy to men. Women who are familiar with life's pleasures are in control of her own pleasures. A woman who isn't afraid to let men know what she wants or likes is an enticing feature to men. Men seem to find this feature to be a real turn on. Some men don't like to play games and when they find a woman who's as strong as they are, it is an accomplishment. Men think that when a woman speaks plainly of her wants, needs and desires it shows that she doesn't play games.

Being able to be direct is a sign of loyalty, and men look for loyalty in their partners. Having a woman that they can count on is a plus in any relationship. Make your man the center of your attention by allowing him the opportunity to be the center of your desire. Then show him how big your desires are.

8. SEX SHOULDN'T BE A CONDITION OF PLEASURES:

Don't ever have sex unless you want to and don't give in to sex until you want it. If you tell him no to sex and he tries to add conditions to your answer, let him go. A woman can control her own agenda and if a man doesn't like it, so what. A man cannot be kept, held or loved any longer by giving in to his requests of sex when you don't want to have sex. Sex isn't the ultimate of what a man wants from a woman. His commitment comes from his interest in you as a woman, and sex is an addition to this interest. Morals and self- respect can help your judgment in making important decisions about sex. Your decisions about sex should be pleasurable, and you should feel good about yourself and about your relationship before sex enters the picture. He'll value you more if you aren't easily accessible or available in sex.

9. DON'T SWEAT THE SMALL STUFF:

Don't get caught up into arguing about the small stuff. In any relationship you will have big and small experiences that neither of you will always agree upon. A rule to always remember: "Don't sweat the small stuff," Rule number two: "It's all small stuff." All relationships are give and take. There will be times that you'll have to give in, and there will be times that he'll have to give in. Don't keep a tally of who gives in the most or the least. Make compromises by taking turns selecting the activity for the day, week or month. What's considered big stuff and what's considered the little stuff are different for all of us. Having the ability to make the distinction is what separates the women from the girls. It's really a matter of mature opinions on most occasions. Just because you gave in to your man doesn't mean that your womanhood is compromised.   Having the power to compromise and feel confident about your decision is a step in the positive direction.

10. ENJOY GOING OUT ALONE:

The chances of meeting someone who you like is always greater when you go out rather alone than sitting at home. Having the need to have a man with you everytime you go out can be discouraging for an interested fellow. Going out with married friends can open up many possibilities of meeting men who are looking for a new adventure with someone just like you. Tagging along can be a new experience and, who knows, you might just meet your better half.

Know what it takes to make you happy.

Chapter 5

TM

PLAYING HIS GAME

Women want reasonably handsome men with personality, integrity, and love along with plenty of material possessions. When a woman finally finds the man that she's been waiting for, she should allow him to feel as though he did the picking and the choosing. Don't give any hints or signs that he's been picked out by you. He'll love a hint of rejection, so don't make yourself to easy for him. Keep a balance between acceptance and rejection. Go back and forth until he's confused with desire. Practice giving yourself and allow it to become a natural reflex. Flirt politely with the warmth of a smile and a welcome glance at all potential prey that you meet. Approximately forty-five percent will flirt back at you.

Smile often and glance regularly at men who have attracted your attention. Focus on each one for about two or three seconds or more. Of the eighty percent that will continue to flirt with you, narrow them down to your personal finalist. Find their eyes watching you, trying to flirt with you, and then focus in on your chosen targets. Any of the guys that continue to flirt and remain in your presence are your best picks. Pick one out of your best picks and began to flirt directly with him. Remain discrete so as not to discourage the others, just in case this one doesn't work out for you. Flirt intensely and consistently, but don't give him all of your time and by all means don't monopolize all of his time.

To assure yourself a few good picks flirt with the others in the same fashion, and then narrow down your choices to the number one pick. Remember that you are doing the picking and choosing without him knowing it. This will build your confidence level to maximum heights and his male ego will remain in tact because he'll think that he did the picking.

Okay. You've made your choice, but suppose he's married or involved in a happy relationship with another woman? Then you'll have to be strong and you'll have to make some important decisions. If he wants to have an affair with you, you will have to remember and understand that he has obligations and other responsibilities which may take priority over you.

Asking him to leave his family, home, and wife won't put you on his most wanted list. Emotions are human and most men would rather have an affair than to pay the price for leaving. Many people automatically blame the other woman, but few men are naturally monogamous and must have more than one woman to feel satisfied entering into an affair with a married man can be painful if you go in blinded. To enjoy this affair be prepared to enjoy the best, but expect the worst also.

TM

Chapter 6

GAMES YOU CAN PLAY

Here are one hundred things that you can do to add spice to your relationship. A real woman will find ways to turn her man on even if he's not accustomed to exotic games of lovemaking that you come up with. These suggestions will help you come a few months this year and maybe even the next year. You can always lengthen this list with your personal best.

1. Wake up before he does and suck his penis until he climaxes.
2. Masturbate him with honey until he climaxes.
3. Ask him to teach you his favorite masturbation technique, let him show you how until he climaxes.
4. Take nude pictures of him masturbating.
5. Let him take pictures of you masturbating.
6. Put a fresh cherry into your vagina and play "Find the Cherry."
7. Lick him up the crack of his ass until he climaxes.
8. Let him lick you all over until you climax.
9. Greet him at the door wearing heels only.

10. Serve him dinner stark naked, with you as the dessert.
11. Let him shave off all your pubic hair.
12. Watch him shave his pubic hair off.
13. Play with his penis as he drives you to work.
14. Suck his penis as he drives you to work.
15. Make passionate love to him before he goes to work.
16. Catch him in the shower and suck him to ecstasy.
17. Put his favorite nude photograph of you into his wallet.
18. Straddle him and make love in the tub.
19. Make sexually erotic phone calls to him at his job.
20. Play with his penis under the table at restaurants.
21. Buy him a dildo and ask him to do the most creative thing to you that he can do.
22. Invite a best girl friend over and surprise him with good sex from the both of you.
23. Buy a massager or a vibrator and massage his penis until he begs you to stop.
24. Write him an erotic letter and put it in his briefcase.
25. Buy a pornographic magazine and read them on long romantic drives.
26. Buy a vibrator and stick it into your own vagina and let him watch you do great things with it.
27. Buy a vibrator and stick it into your butt as he makes love to you.
28. Buy another vibrator and stick one his butt as he makes love to you.
29. Purchase sexy underwear for him.
30. Take him to a dirty movie, then leave there and take him to a live strip show.
31. Make up your own strip show for him.
32. Meet him for lunch in nothing but your undies and a coat.
33. Have sex in someone else's bedroom.
34. Read him a pornographic story in which he's starring.
35. Give him a massage with oils that are sure to turn him on.
36. Have a full-day session of naked extravaganza: sex, photos, and more sex.
37. Suck both of his balls gently at the same time.
38. Masturbate him as he masturbates you and see who climaxes first.

39. Put your tongue up his butt as far as you can.
40. Masturbate him in the back seat of your car.
41. Give him oral sex in the back seat of your car.
42. Give oral sex on the elevator of one of the tallest buildings in your city.
43. Take all of your partner's penis into your mouth.
44. Rape him the next time he doesn't act interested in sex.
45. Tie him up to the bedposts and have your sexual way with him.
46. Let him tie you up and submit to his fantasies.
47. Go without panties to your next social function and allow him to put his finger into your vagina each chance you get.
48. Bite his buttocks as you masturbate him.
49. Bite his nipples during love making.
50. Spell your name on his penis with the tip of your tongue and ask him to figure out the direction of each letter as you spell it.
51. Blindfold him and ask him to guess the flavors that you put onto your vagina. Use several different flavors.
52. Make love in a friend's house, full of guest's in a secret place you've found.
53. Make love in front of a lit fireplace.
54. Make love in a taxi on the way to your destination.
55. Suck his penis while he's talking on the telephone.
56. Hold his penis while he pees, trying to guide it.
57. Allow him to ejaculate in your mouth.
58. Give him a vaginal massage: slowly rub your wet vagina all over his body.
59. Get naked and sit on his face.
60. Lie in the middle of your table and yell to him that dinner is served.
61. Tell him that you love his hard penis.
62. Experiment with a new sexual position each time you have sex.
63. Kiss him and tell him passionately that you love him.
64. Play strip domino. Everytime you score ten points or more, he must remove an item of clothing, your choice.
65. Have him buy a copy of Will The Real Women Please Stand Up.
66. Emerge his penis into a glass of champagne and lick his penis clean.
67. Slide a popsicle into your vagina and slowly lick your own juices from it as he watches you do it over and over again.

68. Challenge him to make mad, passionate love to you for at least six hours in the same night.
69. Let him watch as you slide a cucumber or a dildo all the way into your vagina.
70. Skinny dip in the moonlight with your lover.
71. Send an erotic plant with a sexy note attached.
72. Time each other and see who can make the other climax in the least amount of time.
73. Leave love notes all through your home for him to find.
74. Slip a pair of your favorite panties in his briefcase or lunch box for him to sniff at his leisure.
75. Always smell your best for him. Make it a habit.
76. Keep chilled wine ready for before, during and after sex for sipping.
77. Ask him to strip from head to toe for you to his favorite song.
78. Masturbate YOURSELF as he dances for you.
79. Tell him that you love him again.
80. Everytime that you kiss him make sure it is as passionate as you can get. Lick the roof of his mouth from time to time.
81. Place elegant and sexy photo's or prints in strategic locations.
82. Have a girlfriend take nude pictures of you and give them to him.
83. Stick his big toe into your vagina and then massage his feet.
84. Suck his toes after the foot massage.
85. Lick his eyelids during love making.
86. Be sure to suck his ear lobes often.
87. Stroke his balls as you suck his penis.
88. While waiting in lines together, tell him in a low sexy voice what you plan to do to him when you get home.
89. Use your favorite scents on your bed sheets, pillows and bed covers.
90. Have a mold of his dick professionally made for keep sake.
91. Oil your breasts down with your favorite oils and then give him a breast massage with your breasts.
92. Slide your big toe up his ass and ask him to count to twenty before you take it out.
93. Suck his bottom lip into your mouth at the end of each kiss.
94. Become a real woman, and remain one during sex.

95.   Tell him that you are a real woman and mean it during sex.
96.   Treat him like a real man.
97.   Love yourself more than you love him.
98.   Suck his fingers for no reason at all.
99.   Lick his ears and his eyelids for no reason at all.
100.   Have him to wear a condom, or two, or three, before every sexual encounter.

Giving your man a good time is the object of these games. Don't forget that you're suppose to have as much fun as you can also. Don't short change yourself just to accommodate your man. Make them fun and remember to be innovative by adding your own touch of personality to each.

Keep secrets that are trusted with you.

Chapter 7

OFFICE STRATEGY

If you are a career woman, the best likely place to find a man is in your office or in connection with your professional surroundings. Relationships on the job are real life relationships and are very common. Being interested in your supervisor can be either efficient or inefficient. Values go a long way with your boss if you are always on time, efficient, and organized. Having a relationship with you might jeopardize him. He won't want to jeopardize your efficiency by having a relationship with you. On the other hand, if you aren't efficient, are always late, full of mistakes and very untidy he won't waste his time either and there's little chance that he'll want to keep you for his sexual entertainment. He'll conclude you're just as tacky with your relationships. Remain efficient, hard-working and every now and then come in late so as not to draw unnecessary attention.

Don't dress up too often because you'll embarrass him. Skirts too short and blouses cut too low will attract unnecessary attention from him and his colleagues. When selecting clothes to wear to the office, don't confuse evening wear or weekend wear with office wear. There is a difference unless your job has a dress code in force. Be familiar with career dress codes.

When attempting to seduce the boss, be prepared for a long-term exercise.

He'll have to see you in a different way than he normally does. He'll have to adjust his view to see a sexually attractive woman. Chat with him frequently and he'll construct a picture of you and your personality in his mind. This will allow him to begin to become familiar with you in his mind without him knowing it. You'll get a chance to get to know him better also.

If you've taken your boss through all of the necessary stages and he still doesn't give in to you, he'll need a push or something to help him find you attractive. Show up at work one day in your prettiest dress and go to him with a problem that you need his help with. Invent a problem if there isn't one. The main objective is to get his attention. This must be a story so intense and so mind- boggling that it will merit a place away from the office to discuss it with him properly. Getting him out of the office will be the first goal, so that he will genuinely realize that you are attractive, sensuous, and pleasant company. Don't worry, once you get him away from the office he'll react in the normal masculine way. Once he gets relaxed and lets his guard down it'll be your chance to respond to his normal masculine instincts.

Don't talk about work or office because he'll be in the boss role and you'll lose all the personal attention you've worked so hard to get. Once you've begun your new relationship with your boss you must never allow it to surface in the work place, no matter how hot and passionate you both feel. You must remain completely professional at work. This could work in your favor because the fact that he won't be able to touch you will turn him on even more. You don't want the affair to become idle office gossip or a company scandal. Don't give him a reason to drop you or fire you due to negative talk.

Don't get so weak that you sit on his lap for dictation. Don't stare endlessly at him or parts of his body while at work. And if he insist give him a tiny kiss and leave it at that only if no one is around. If he's married and other women or his wife calls, remain professional at all costs; resist eye rolling and negative responses. Remember when you decided to have an affair with him you also chose his wife and children. Don't allow your attitude to send him back into her arms.

If all the men at your job are married or too old fashioned for you, look elsewhere. Don't waste precious time toying with men who don't interest you.

TM

Chapter 8

WINNING TECHNIQUES

Men lack confidence. So, if you're interested in one, you'd better send out obvious signals of your attraction or he'll miss them all. In a room full of people, (mainly men) one of the best seduction techniques is to scan the room and then flirtatiously go for what you know.

Stare frequently at your choice. And with each stare, lengthen its time. Short glances and small encouraging smiles have terrific affects on men. Men usually eye women, not women to men, so turning the tables on them flatters men tremendously. Lingering, sly looks allow you to show interest without being committed to anyone. It will open the way for him to approach you and start the conversation later. Don't get all wild and slavered over him when he displays a coolness. Drop a hint of your interest every now and then so that he won't lose his nerve and decide not to talk to you. Even if he tends to be unsure still give him a chance and he'll show you his appreciation with great responses.

To make an extra impression on the man you've chosen, provoke an intelligent argument after listening to him for a while. No man gets his adrenalin flowing for a woman who always agrees with him. Don't get too worked up or excited or too overbearing. Keep your cool and be pleasantly contradictory. You'll find that he's suddenly given all of his attention to you, and he's found an excitement while talking to you. You'll find that you've become that needed challenge that he doesn't find in other females and he'll give extra effort with you.

The stage is now set for challenge, reaction, attraction, and seduction. Men are obviously flattered by women who run to their every call, but they're intrigued and turned on by women who won't. Your personal openness in the way that you approach men is up to you, but be ready to back up whatever you do or say. If you get overly aggressive with a man don't scream wolf if he wants to fuck you. He's only answering and responding to your love gestures. Don't lead a man on and don't make him think that you are an easy lay. You'll end up physically abused or emotionally torn. Resist laughing too loud when you're surrounded by a host of men. Men will not see you as sexy or attractive, they will see you as silly.

Women who attract men regularly are women who look fantastic, encouraging, promising, sexy, and distinctively different with something in reserve. This woman who has reserved secrets is a woman with something that arouses men to a challenge. She'll be the one who's sexy without being overbearing or a nymphomaniac. She'll be vocal without being too outspoken, and she'll know when to open her seductive eyes and close her mouth as she listens to one of his ego-tripping tales.

A man loves a woman who listens to his stories of himself and his personal achievements. It helps to build his ego when he tells stories of his rejections. Be positive and stroke his ego when he's showing signs of low self-esteem.

Regularly compliment him, and as you do, stroke his back slightly, this will give him goose bumps. Stroke his side burns and say nice things as you stroke. If you smoke, gently hold his wrist as he lights up your cigarette. You can also pretend to read his palm as you gently stroke his hand. This will send messages of comfort throughout his body. Stimulating a man can be quite simple if you use creativity and imagination.

Dancing can bring about hidden seductiveness also. Dancing gives women an excuse to be seductive. Just as respectability can be achieved from clinging on his arm. A woman can grind, roll, touch and moan without anyone knowing. She can masturbate him and dance with him at the same time. She can use her thighs when dancing and cause him to have an erection.

You don't have to be a whore to be attracted to a man who you want but don't know. In a busy store, airport or grocery store you can have a man to help you choose deodorants, colognes, or even shaving creams by asking for his help in your selections. Asking him to sniff wrists, arms, necks, of even your hair is a great turn on for him.

If you see a stranger who you are attracted to, be very subtle and ask where you might buy a hat or any other piece of clothing that he has on for your brother. Other tactics are asking directions, the time, or something brief that needs a lengthy explanation. He'll notice that you are a good listener.

In applying these techniques you are still left with dignity, and you aren't being pushy and overbearing. The actual invitation will appear to be his and the fun of it all is that he doesn't realize he's been set up to react a certain way.

Many women believe that cooking a four-course meal will get the man that she wants. What will get the man that a woman wants is confidence in herself as a woman. Letting him know that you want him will get a better response than a dimly lit dinner. Stealing time to cook and prepare a meal for him takes away from valuable intimacy. Besides, you're likely to run him away because men feel that woman are looking for a husband when they prepare elaborate dinners for him. Be sure you're tidy, warm, cordial and most of all, feminine. Keep a couple of bottles of wine and a nice bottle of liquor around. Have pizza, chinese food, or cheese and crackers or even finger foods, but don't overdo it on food. You want him and he wants you, not your food. Dressing sexy is best when you are trying to romance your man. A frilly low cut blouse and long tight skirt will work. Wearing no under garments is nice and sexy also. Tight slacks with a glittery tank top are provocative. Be sure hair and make-up are fresh and always complimentary. Invest in kinky underwear for later in the relationship to heighten sensuality.

Early in the relationship, play the sexy, desirable, innocent girl; not the fully experienced one who's ready for mad sex. Do everything to make him comfortable. Don't go to the bathroom to finish make-up and tell him to fix his own drink. Remain in his presence, hang his jacket and pour his drink for him. Ask if he would like something to eat and if he says no don't let it bother you. Keep the mood relaxed and positive.

Once you've done everything that's needed to assure he's comfortable, you can relax. Now that both of you are relaxed let the relationship begin.

With these winning techniques you're going to be the apple of several men's eyes, so be ready to enjoy pampering and let the feelings flow. Men that I interviewed said that they appreciate women that are sure of themselves, and not overbearing or cocky. This doesn't mean to be so submissive that you began to feel like his slave. No one wants a mate that is a sucker for love. It doesn't help either person's self esteem, nor does it increase the passion. Being a puppet is not being considerate or in love. Men might adore your whining and helpless features in the beginning of the relationship because of their male ego, but after a few weeks of this weakness, he'll soon tire and began to look for a woman that has it more together than you. Most men want women that can carry their weight and still connect with their feminine ways. They also attracted to women that will not appear to be a future handicap to their pocket or their time. Don't forget to carry little objects to constantly appear to be prepared. These types of gadgets or handy tools can serve your needs as well as his. I've listed a few things to help you get it all together.

1. Miniature Flashlights can be purchased at hardware stores
2. Mace can be purchased at gas stations, car dealerships and some grocery stores
3. Handkerchiefs
4. Mirror that are tiny and easy to pack in your purse
5. Tweezers to stay ahead of the unwanted hair game.
6. Fingernail clippers
7. A small note pad should be a natural part of your attire to take numbers or to send notes to a man that you admire from afar.
8. Small purses are attractive and feminine as well as conservative on a beautifully dressed woman.
9. Breath mints, toothbrush and toothpaste for freshening your breath.
10. Extra panties are a girl's best friend, so that you can leave a pair for him to sniff after you've gone or to make a fresh change when needed through out an active or busy day.
11. Small, delicate gadgets of your personal choice are handy also.

SPECIAL NOTE:
Don't let your items become too bulky or noisy. No real woman needs to attract unnecessary attention by clinging and clanging on her entrance. Your items must be subtle and slightly noticeable. Use items that really serve a purpose and that will help you to narrow your list down.

Chapter 9

BECOMING A SENSUOUS WOMAN

After years of research, I have found that some of the most confusing and disappointed experiences of females have been sensual or sexual.

Some of my most tantalizing, earth shaking, shrieking, faint occurring moments have been sexual. Once you have had your first sexual encounter, it becomes an inescapable part of joy. Our sexual differences are mentally given to us from birth until the day we die.

We, as females, owe it to ourselves to understand our own sexuality, sensuality, sexual needs, and desires. To began to understand why it's so important to be a sensuous woman, I've covered several topics that I've found to be the most beneficial. After talking to hundreds of woman about sexuality, I've found that each of them have one thing in common when it comes to the men we love. Women want to keep men by pleasing them ultimately.

Being sensuous does not mean to be weak. To be soft and fragile is a necessity. You must appear to enjoy the role of the so-called weaker sex. The luxury of having doors opened, chairs pulled out, packages carried, and the pleasures of being able to cry openly when we, as females, feel like it is a natural part of being a woman. The benefits of sensuality can sometimes be very rewarding. The joy of giving everything of ourselves to the men we love, and the delight of receiving great gifts like diamonds, minks, and rubies are all rewards for succeeding in sensuality.

You can consider yourself lucky if you already possess sensuous qualities. All women will have a chance to discover their sensuous selves. So go ahead, enjoy yourself in bed, have orgasms, lots of them. And don't go through guilt trips afterwards. Women are now realizing for the first time that we are not just receptacles for sperm. Our bodies are NOT just a place to store embryos.

Good love making should become the number one priority with you and your man. Good love-making awakens you emotionally, spiritually, and sensuously by relaxing your mind, muscles and spirit.

Enjoy the sensuous aspects of love-making. because it makes you forget your worries for a while. It aids in attaining restful sleep and is one of the OLDEST pleasures in this world.

In sensuous love-making you will not be alone. Your companion should be one that is compassionate, sensitive, admiring, and wants to give and take you completely to new sexual heights. You can get all the loving that's needed if you unwrap your sensuality. Work with every ounce of you to make things work in your favor. Don't deprive yourself unnecessarily because you can change your negative sexual and emotional patterns. I have, and I've found an unleashed happiness that has been long awaited.

Some of us come into full sexuality without effort. However, for most women becoming a completely sensuous woman is often a difficult process. In the past, very few have succeeded. But with this book and a desire to learn your success rate will increase. We, as females, owe this to ourselves.

If you are not sensuous, you are cheating yourself and you need to know it. Don't frustrate yourself by blaming. Be sensuous by loving your body and enjoying who you are. Be sensuous by being smart, intelligent and aware of who you are. Be sensuous with your actions. Think, walk, and speak sensuous, and most of all look discretely sensuous.

By achieving the correct response patterns, sensuality within you will pour outward, yet remain conservative. In other words, your sensuous techniques will show, be used in a positive way and remain intact to be used over and over again on the men of your choice.

To become sensuous and remain sensuous, we as women must practice our sensuality techniques on a daily basis. In these times, women of all ages can be sensuous. Unleashing that pent up passion that's waiting to be freed is the first step. Forget the myths of nice girls don't do that. I've been told more than once by guys of all ages that men want a nice young lady. Yes, a nice young lady, but with whore- like qualities. Every man wants a fantastic bed partner without inhibitions and hang ups. Executives, school teachers, secretaries, lawyers, doctors, therapists, and others can all be good girls by everyone's standards, but to her man she needs to be the good little whore. Go on girls, be a whore for your man, and a very good one, too. Catch on fire, concentrate on sex, think of your satisfaction and climax with your lover. When the sensuality of it all sets in, you will feel much more secure as a woman, and a sensuous woman at that.

"Hmmm," I thought. If this program works for me and is successful then why wouldn't it work for all women. I began a few test cases, like my best friend Larna. Larna met men frequently, but could never seem to keep them interested in her. They always left her after three or four weeks. I set out to find out what the problem was. After a few weeks of girl talk and comparisons of her dates, I found out that she was only going out with men whom she thought had money. That was okay, but, why did they leave so quickly? One problem that needed fixing was once Larna got the man who she wanted she had to keep him. We began my Will The Real Women Please Stand Up program. She found that my program enabled her to keep her lovers coming back for more. Each time they came (smile), they left fulfilled and she reaped the rewards and awards sexually, physically, mentally, and financially.

**Women enjoy the happiness they give.
Men enjoy the happiness they feel.**

Chapter 10

BECOMING A SENSUOUS LEADER

WHAT IT TAKES

Seeing that you can please a man sexually and otherwise, is the biggest turn-on of all. Giving a little kiss with sincerity and passion can entice a man more than hours of sensuous lovemaking. Women should be more aware of the power that they have over men. Any woman can be the woman that a man really wants. All it takes is how you, as a sensuous leader, can make a man feel in love, sex and relationships. Here are some helpful hints:

1. <u>LOOK FOR WAYS TO IMPROVE YOURSELF</u> through reading asking questions, or getting additional training. Don't rest on what you've learned in the past. Get in the spirit of working continuously to improve your relationship with your man.

2. <u>BE SERVICE ORIENTED</u> no matter what you do for a living. Ask and help your man, don't be selfish with your talents.

3. <u>RADIATE</u> <u>WITH</u> <u>POSITIVE</u> <u>ENERGY</u> and avoid being negative or treating your man negatively.

4. <u>BELIEVE</u> <u>IN</u> <u>OTHER</u> <u>PEOPLE</u> by seeing good in others. Affirm your man's worth by believing in him.

5. <u>BALANCE</u> <u>YOUR</u> <u>LIFE</u> between your work, home, and community. Don't be too busy for your man.

6. <u>SEE</u> <u>LIFE</u> <u>AS</u> <u>AN</u> <u>ADVENTURE</u> by seeing each day in a fresh, new and exciting way. Do exciting things with your lover on a regular basis.

7. <u>VALUE</u> <u>DIFFERENCE</u> by realizing that your way is not always the right way, nor is it the only possible way. Alternatives are exciting, not a threat.

8. <u>TAKE</u> <u>CARE</u> <u>OF</u> <u>YOURSELF</u> physically through exercise. Be healthy intellectually by praying often, or simple meditating is inspirational.

9. <u>LEAVE</u> <u>A</u> <u>POSITIVE</u> <u>IMPRESSION</u> by giving good news last. End conversations or news on an up note.

10. <u>DON'T</u> <u>GOSSIP</u>. Women can't afford to. Love yourself and, in turn, you will be able to love others.

Chapter 11

TM

TAKING CARE OF YOU:

<u>YOU'VE</u> <u>GOT</u> <u>THE</u> <u>POWER</u>

The business of taking care of you is in the hands of you more so than anyone else. You've got the power to be the best that you can be if you start with a little positive personal adjustment. The first step is to turn your dream into a clearly defined goal. This may not be as impossible as it sounds. Our choices are often influenced by the values and expectations of others which, however well-intended, may not be the right choice for us. Our heart's desire may be different from what others expect of us. To find out what you really want in a man, set aside private time to jot down your ideas which will in turn force you to see things clearer. What would you truly like to have? Can the man who you have or the one who you are looking for help you to attain your goals? Write down all your dreams, even if at first they sound unattainable or ridiculous.

Don't be afraid to aim high and stretch yourself. If you aren't challenged by your man you may lose your enthusiasm. Practice aiming high because you'll probably accomplish more than if you lower your expectations and make them realistic. However, strangely unrealistic expectations can be a form of self-sabotage. Don't expect to find your Knight in Shining Armor in a day or even a week. It may take longer; just remember to stick to your list of requirements for your dream boat.

Your wish list will probably have enough on it to fill a life time. You must narrow it down to what matters most to you, what really excites you. Look for these qualities in the man of your dreams and go after him. To help set your priorities, write down the things that you like in a man and the things that most men have said that they like in you, then compare the list. You might find that there is room for improvement needed in you.

Don't be afraid to accept the fact that you may have flaws. Be a woman about it and accept your shortcomings by working to improve yourself. And don't expect the man of your dreams to be flawless because no one is perfect, not even you.

SELF ASSESSMENT

Many of us take our greatest abilities so much for granted that we don't even know we have them. To bring your personal assets into focus, take inventory on several sheets of paper. On the paper, list your known good points and remember not to be modest. Divide one of the sheets of paper into two columns. On the left, list everything special or unusual you've done- starting with childhood, if you can remember (at least try). On the right note the traits that these reflect. Now, compare the columns with your first sheet. You're almost certain to spot abilities that you didn't know you had. Last, but not the least, an ideal goal to catch the man of your dreams includes a plan to strengthen your personal weaknesses. Strengthening your personal weaknesses can be beneficial to meeting the man of your dreams. It will not only improve you as a person, but also help to improve your standards therefore helping you to reach higher goals and finding that lucky someone who has been waiting to find you all his life.

<u>STAY</u> <u>FLEXIBLE</u>

Don't under estimate your ability to improve yourself no matter how many times you've already tried. If you really want to change yourself to the better, begin now. Don't put it off another day. DO IT FOR YOU!!! By mapping out a plan and being flexible as well as resourceful, your dream will become a reality. Don't be so strict with yourself, loosen up and go with the flow. It is equally important to be aware of what you don't want in a man. Remember that you are becoming a confident and sensual woman, which means that you don't have to settle for just any man and/or behavior that you don't care for.

*** CAUTION: BEING TOO STRICT IN THE BEDROOM
CAN LEAD HIM TO AFFAIRS**

Take long bubble baths.

Chapter 12

FEMALE MAINTENANCE:

BASIC HYGIENE

Americans understand the logic behind keeping the body clean and fresh. Deciding to take a bath or shower only on special days or occasions, or in an emergency is tacky and unethical. No one wants to make love to a woman with offensive body odors. Contrary to all of the myths, hype and commercialism, basic hygiene is not achieved through the process of wearing clean underwear or taking a bath. It takes responsible awareness of your own personal attributes to bring out the personal bacteria-sensor in you.

FRESHNESS

A shower in the morning will be enough to last throughout the day. For an after work date, you will need higher standards of hygiene, especially if intimacy will be involved. If you practice basic feminine hygiene, even the so-called hookers bath will adequately suffice. All that's needed is a basin to wash your vital parts. Even if love-making is not on your agenda, you should still take sanitary precautions before your date. Passion may develop at any time, so good grooming reflects your hygiene to your partner and it doesn't damage your self-esteem either.

During your monthly periods, keep tampons and sanitary napkins available. Change often to keep that fresh feeling. If you don't change often enough odor can build up and be quite offensive and unpleasant. Bad or unpleasant odors in the love section can be very disgusting and unfeminine. All women should have a gynecologist to conference with at least once every six months to a year, especially if you are sexually active.

We at one point and time in our lives need help from Mother Nature. We know that herpes, body odors, bad breath, or a cold sore on the lip now denotes bad grooming. Flavored douches that are supposed to save a troubled relationship do less than inspire one. A perspective that is practical, sensible and desirable is at the least necessary.

Feminine hygiene is presex courtesy that all women who are sexually active should adhere to. Basic hygiene makes us more enticing to the opposite sex. An investment into your feminine hygiene as a woman is worth the time, effort, and trouble.

A normal healthy woman who bathes regularly and is conscientiously aware of basic hygiene, has no need for the industrial gimmicks. Most woman feel that vaginal deodorants are either rash causing, over perfumed, or they diminish arousal instead of assisting with the production of it. The wisdom of nature has prepared our bodies to smell clean with low maintenance and with sex comes an intoxicating aroma that should always be considered natural and wholesome. If you come across a man who would rather smell perfumes or flavored body parts before he'll acknowledge you, beware; he's interested in you for the wrong reasons.

SOME BASICS TO REMEMBER:
1. Prior to bathing, slough off dead skin cells with a bristle brush. This will help to bring smoothness to your skin.
2. If skin is super dry, avoid basic bubble bath because it depletes   skin of its natural oils.
3. Intensify experiences by placing candles around the tub .
4. Try to layer fragrances. Add your favorite bath version to your tub

and after drying off splash on your favorite perfume. You'll radiate a sensuous allure.

5. Moisturize immediately after bathing. This will seal in water that skin has absorbed. "Oatmeal baths are good for relaxing itchy dry skin."

6. Never soak in a very hot bath for more than twenty minutes. This could dehydrate skin. Best water temperature is 85 degrees.

7. A terrific detoxifier is a mud bath mix.

8. Use a pumice stone on feet, loofah on knees, elbows and bikini line. This will make your body feel like silk.

9. The best rule to remember is basic hygiene should be a daily practice for all sexually active women. It's for the health of it.

Whatever works for someone else, may not work for you.

Chapter 13

PERSONAL APPEARANCE:

<u>MARKETING YOU</u>

Remembering that you are a product to be marketed as well as packaged will help your personal appearance. You don't have to be Elizabeth Taylor or Tina Turner, but you'd better be attractive and have a pleasing personality. You'll never get into a man's heart let alone his head unless you are pleasantly attractive and appear interesting to him. Many of the ideas listed are areas that women need to pay more attention to. If you find that you need to work on these areas, begin as soon as possible to strengthen these weaknesses. Correcting these areas will start a new attitude about your appearance.

Before you can improve your appearance you must be able to recognize your faults. Don't be afraid to re-evaluate yourself. The best way to do this is to list questions about yourself that you would ask another female. Pay close attention to areas that you personally think need extra work or attention. If you think that these areas needs extra work or attention they probably do.

FASHION

Collecting fashion magazines, articles and pictures will help you to coordinate and suggest ideas to the existing wardrobe that you have. By devoting some time and effort to your appearance on a regular basis, you'll be able to find flattering clothes that compliment your finer points. Seeing a new and improved you in a short time only takes some concentrated effort.

Another way to enhance your appearance or flatter your figure is to go to department stores, boutiques, or even discount stores with a friend and try on new types of clothing that you always wondered what you would look like in. Get away from your figure faults. Work with your good points. Be fashion conscious, dress for success, but don't let fashion enslave you. Be a trendsetter. When everyone is wearing baggy pants and loose blouses, be the one to wear tight pants and a skimpy blouse. You'll turn heads, especially men's heads. Most men are attracted to the colors that you wear. In a survey of one hundred men, seventy percent chose blue as their favorite color, so try to wear plenty of blue. Don't buy clothes because they're practical, they tend to look cheap. Unless it jumps off the rack at you, try not to buy it. When trying on clothes, look at yourself in the mirror at all angles, sitting, standing, squatting, and bending. Observe strengths and weaknesses as you walk. Does the clothing lie smooth or slide up. Is its maintenance easy or difficult? Does your skirt hike up in the back or front? How clean do you look? Is your skin smooth and beautiful? Are your hands rough and harsh looking? Do your teeth have stains and discolorations? Are your nails chipped and/or unmanicured? Are your shoes scuffed or scarred, run over or dirty? Do your clothes appear dingy or faded? Are you wearing clothes that fit too tight or are they obviously too big? Don't be guilty of any of these things. If you are, start working to improve today. Be aware of your weaknesses; men certainly will.

UNDERWEAR

Never, ever be caught with dirty underwear, or underwear held together by safety pins. Bras held together by safety pins are one of the worst things to do. Invest in new ones and throw the old ones away. In the past, clean underwear was mainly suggested in case of an accident precaution that your parents always made sure you abided by. You took a bath whether you thought you needed it or not, and with this bath you had fulfilled the main requirement of cleanliness. Since women and sex have replaced American's favorite pastime, the care and grooming of our bodies has become a national symbol of wholesomeness. With television commercials, radio, movies and talk show hosts advertising flavored edible underwear, our society can't help but think basic hygiene.

Remember that very brief, thin underwear looks good on men and women. The more sensuous, the more inviting.

PERFUMES, COLOGNES, AND FRAGRANCES

Unless you (or your man) have allergic reactions to perfumes, colognes, or fragrances, please wear it. Cheap imitations are simply that, "cheap imitations." To be complimented or asked the name of the perfume you are wearing should be taken as a well deserved compliment. If you are asked more than several times a day, it is usually a very good indication that you've hit on a good fragrance, one that compliments your body chemistry.

HOW TO WEAR PERFUME?

To get the most from your perfume, perfumes should be worn on all pulse spots of your body. Apply perfume and cologne on your skin, rather than your clothes. Chemicals in fragrances may weaken fabric or change its color.
* Don't overdo it, your favorite cologne may clash with a room full of other smells so dab lightly in various places.
* Choose a perfume or fragrance that compliments your natural body odor.
* Don't mix too many different smells like deodorant, lotions powders, perfumes.   All on the same body can be quite repulsive.   Many companies make lotions, body oils, perfumes, soaps and bath gels of the same scents to help women in choosing.   You can find odorless deodorants.

WHERE TO APPLY PERFUMES

1. Ankles	2. Palms
3. Back of your knees	4. Bend of your elbows
5. Behind the ears	6. base of the throat
7. Bosom	8. Inside of your wrists
9. Between your thighs	

Fragrance is seductive, and it really gets a woman noticed, but a quick spritz is not the way to go. To make a definite and lasting impression, here are more simple techniques:

1. **TWIRL!** spray eau de toilette in the air , and then spin in the mist of it all. The misty molecules of your spray should settle all over your awaiting body, hair, and clothing...yummy.
2. **ULTIMATE ALLURE!** lightly scent cotton ball or a hankie and stuff it in your bra, pocket or glove.
3. **RE-SCENT!** just as you would touch up your lipstick, touch up your fragrance. This combats fade out and olfactory overload because your nose doesn't register odor once you've used it.
4. **CAN'T AFFORD THE REAL THING!** less expensive bath oils and moisturizing versions are potent and REALLY last! Dab on the above spots mentioned the same as you would perfume.

A FEW MORE TIPS

~check out new Eau De Perfumes. These fall between toilet water and perfume in strength, but are much less expensive.

~ use matching bath and body products to layer your fragrance.

~multi-floral and oriental types stay vital the longest, and are the most arousing.

~avoid scent buying just prior to menstruation, when your sense of smell is weakest. (The birth control pill is said to also alter odor-detecting ability)

~hair is a fabulous perfume vehicle. Mix a few drops with your conditioner then run it through your hair.

~the best application time is right after you shower; your open pores will soak up the aroma.

~dab petroleum on your pulse points, and then apply perfume directly to these areas.

~apply perfume and cologne before putting on your jewelry. The alcohol and oils in your favorite scent can cause a cloudy film on both real gold and costume jewelry.

~don't stick to one fragrance all year-long, because temperatures affect the intensity of fragrance. Use heavy scents and oils in winter but lighter fragrances in smaller quantities during the summer.

Some questions you should ask yourself:

How does wearing fragrance make you feel ?

Do you wear fragrance for yourself or other people ?

How often do wear fragrances ?
How many different fragrances do you own ?
When do you wear your fragrance ?
How often do you switch fragrances ?
When was the last time you purchased a new fragrance ?

NEATNESS COUNTS

Even if you are a little on the wild side, the punk rock type person or the mild, meek and mannered type person, you should still be neat, clean, and attractive in your appearance. No runs in your hosiery, no holes in your socks, no faded fake earrings, no running mascara, no smudges in your make-up, no smeared lip stick, no scuffed handbags, no missing buttons, no broken zippers, no threads dangling and never wear day-old make-up. Freshen up and clean old make-up off on a daily basis. Remember to touch up frequently. Throw away torn or faded dresses or blouses. Use as cleaning rags only.

SHOES

When wearing shoes, flats can be worn in your true size, but heels should be at least 1/2 size larger for comfort. This method also eliminates corns and calluses, which are not a pretty sight on a woman or man. Shoes on a woman should display a sense of purity and cleanliness. When wearing shoes you'll be wearing a lot, consider choosing a pair made of leather or woven fabric. These materials breath and are usually more comfortable than shoes made of synthetic materials.

Wear shoes that compliment your feet. A friend of yours might be able to wear sling backs because of the size and shape of her foot, but you might not be able to. Make sure your shoe wardrobe includes a pair of shoes in a neutral color that goes well with a wide range of clothing colors.

Be selective, and true to yourself, as well as complimentary.

Shoes should be:

1. Clean and shining.
2. Neat and fitting.
3. Never wear shoes too tight or too small.
4. Heels should be well kept, clean, polished and even.
5. Toes of shoes should be well kept and unscuffed.

HAVING HEEL APPEAL

Women have their own interpretation of heels. They think of heels as their stature, pedestals and they wear them as a sensual statement. High heels entice some men because of the sexuality they reveal. Heel appeal gives legs curves and elegance. Women with long legs can create dramatic effects when donning a pair of high heels. High heels give an added height to the frame of a woman's body.

NAILS

Keep your fingernails and toenails well manicured and polished, even if it's only a clear coat of polish. Be sure to make it a habit to keep under nails clean as possible. Beautiful nails are a plus. Don't forget to polish your toe nails also. Remember to wear nail polish that compliments your natural skin tone. Wearing the same color as your best friend may not be the best choice for you. What looks good on her may not compliment you. Remain an individual by wearing what looks good on you.

Caring for Your Hands and Nails

1. When nails chip excessively, it may be caused by the use of nail polish remover. Leave your nails unpainted for a few days to see if the condition improves.
2. When you're preparing anything with lemon and vegetable juices, which contain acids that are hard on your fingernails, rinse your hands often under cool running water.
3. To break the habit of nail biting or cuticle chewing, carry a tube of cuticle cream with you. Whenever you start to nibble, put the cream on your cuticles instead. You'll promote healthy nails and break yourself of a bad habit.
4. To prevent nail polish from thickening, store it in the refrigerator.
5. To rescue nail polish that has become hardened or gummy, place the bottle into a pan of boiling water for a few seconds to get the polish flowing smoothly again.
6. A light color nail polish gives your hands the illusion of being longer and more graceful.
7. Use a diamond-dust nail file or an emery board. File nails in one direction only.

8. To prevent nail polish bottle tops from sticking, rub the inside of the cap and the neck of the bottle with a thin layer of petroleum jelly.

HAIR

Designer clothing, perfectly applied make-up, and fine jewelry are all wasted if your hair looks greasy, dull, or messy. Fortunately, no one needs an expensive professional hair salon or expensive hair products to have hair that looks professionally cared for and styled. With the right techniques for shampooing, drying, and styling your hair, it can be one of your most attractive features.

Invest in a good haircut and hair style that compliments the beautiful features of your face. Every hair style is not intended to be worn by every face. Be different, yet complimentary. The basic cut is the key to an attractive hair style If the cut is not right, no matter what you do, the style will not last; and it will not flatter your face, nor will it look fresh and neat on a daily basis.

Unless you are a part of the leper colony, underarms and legs are sheared of any hair. Try not to wear that mustache that keeps peaking out. Get electrolysis if needed. Pubic hair can be trimmed to help keep unwanted odors to a minimum. Be sure to trim or shave any long hairs that peek out from your panties and bikini's. It's unattractive and barbaric to present yourself with hairs hanging out of your underwear.

As far as the rest of your body hair, it's up to you whether you trim or shave it. Don't get carried away with trying to remove any hair other than the underarms and legs, or obvious pubic hairs. Trying to shave the hair surrounding your navel or hair on your nipples is not what we call unwanted hair. Once you begin to shave hair from these places it will come back in triplicate. Whatever hair you decide to remove be consistent and aware of unsightly hair. Women tend to become very relaxed in such things when they are involved in a long-term relationship. This is being personally inconsiderate. The abrasive stubble can ruin a once beautiful situation.

If you have dandruff, use a good dandruff shampoo. Try the following treatment every two weeks: Section your hair and rub your scalp with a cotton pad saturated with plain rubbing alcohol. Let the alcohol dry, then brush your hair and rinse thoroughly with warm water, but don't shampoo.

You can check with your local pharmacist on which product or brand is best to use for your type of hair. After shampooing, rinse your hair with cool water to seal in the moisture in the hair shafts.

~To distribute the natural oils in your hair, bend over and brush your scalp and hair from back to front until the scalp tingles; then massage your scalp with your fingertips.

~To cut down on static electricity, dampen your hairbrush before brushing hair. Avoid using a brush on wet hair, because it is subject to breakage.

~To get a fuller look to your hair style, bend over so that your hair falls forward and blow the underneath layers dry first.

~To perk up curly permed hair between shampoos, lightly lightly mist your hair with fresh water and push the curls into place with your fingers.

~dull, lifeless hair can be a sign of a poor diet. Try cutting down on cholesterol and fats.

~Wait at least 48 hours after coloring hair before you shampoo it. Every time you wet hair you open the cuticle, so give hair time to seal in the color.

~Hair sprays, mousses, gels, and other styling aids build up over time, despite judicious shampooing and rinsing. If you find this happening, buy a clarifier, which removes product build-up without stripping essential oils. Make your own by mixing one (1) part vinegar with twenty (20) parts water.

EYES

Your eyes are the windows to the soul.   They tell the world who you are.

Some techniques used to add allure and ravish eyes:
1. Apply regular foundation over the entire lid area. This helps everything else adhere.
2. Pluck your eyebrows from underneath, then fill in the eye shadow that's a shade lighter than your natural color. Some women draw on the shape they want before they pluck or   after they pluck.
3. Use mascara on your lashes. Then, if you need more depth or thickness, paste one or two rows of false lashes on top.
4. Warm a spoon, slightly with a lighter, then curl real or fake lashes over the spoon to bead and blend. (professional model's secret)
5. Gently pull your skin around your eyes outward as you sweep back liquid liner across your upper lid line.
6. Define the bottom of your eyes with brown eye pencil, both underneath and inside them.
7. Dot concealer one tone lighter than your skin over dark circles that usually surround the eyes.   Smooth in to blend.

8. Use two shades of eyebrow pencil to make your brow color look more natural.

MORE WAYS TO RAVISH EYES

~Use your eyes as a flirtatious vehicle to send signs, signals, and gestures in positive ways.

~Healthy habits such as placing sliced raw potatoes over and under eye bags for ten minutes can help to aide your assets. The chemical composition draws the excess water from the skin that causes puffiness.

~A Hawaiian trick for thicker lashes; apply a bit of castor oil with fingers before bed. This encourages new growth.

~Plucking is a must! Try icing before you pluck to ease pain.

~You can use an ordinary number 2 pencil to fill in brows.

~Revive tired eyes by covering with cucumbers, or kiwi slices (leave on for ten minutes)

~Do try subtle colored contacts for a change in eye color.

~Invest in good make-up brushes. This will help to provide foolproof make-up.

~To make the whites of your eyes appear whiter, line your lower lashes with a deep-blue color stick.

~To bring out deep-set eyes, apply a light, frosted shadow on both your lids and brow bone, using a darker shade in the eyelid crease.

~Avoid matching the color of your eye shadow to the exact shade of your eyes. The colors will cancel each other out, making your eyes look drab.

~Protect your eyelashes with a thin coat of waterproof mascara whenever you're outdoors.

~For thick looking lashes, apply mascara and let it set for a few minutes. Then add a little more mascara to the tips. If you use an eyelash curler, curl the lashes before you add mascara to the tips.

~Applying fresh mascara over the old will make your lashes brittle. Be sure to use mascara remover to clean your lashes before going to bed.

~When your mascara begins to dry out, run hot water over the tube for a few minutes to soften the remaining mascara inside.

~Limit the use of eye drops during the summer, because overuse can be harmful.

~Small eyes can be made to look larger by applying eye shadow under your lower lashes starting at the center of the eye and blending to the outer corner. Sweep the color along the brow bone out to the side of your eye.

*The spirit behind your eyes is only one of the many keys to unlocking sensuality. Using your eyes as a creative and seductive tool can produce some of the most pleasurable moments to remember.

SKIN

Your skin is a bellweather to your overall health. If you're not healthy, it will be reflected in your complexion. But that doesn't mean you should neglect your skin if you're feeling fine.

Some easy ways to clear up your skin problems:

1. Don't play with it, put notes on mirrors to remind yourself not to pick it.
2. Try not to touch or lean your cheek on the cradle of the phone, because particles of food or secretions from the mouth may be there.
3. To flush out impurities, drink lots of water.
4. Never go to sleep before removing make-up. If you hate to sleep with a naked face, dust lightly with pressed powder and blush.
5. Get at least eight hours of sleep per night.
6. Use oil-free powder during exercise if you must wear make-up so that your pores won't clog. Clean your face with astringent after your workout.
7. To diffuse stress, take vitamin C.
8. Avoid laundry detergents with sodium laurylsulfite (pimple-producing ingredient).
9. Take ibuprofen when cyst like pimples appear. This also reduces the inflammation.
10. To calm facial redness, take ice breaks twice a day for two minutes.Place cold towels or towels with crushed ice gently against the face for several minutes each morning. You'll feel revitalized as well asfresh and perky.
11. Switch to low dose or triphasol birth control pills.
12. Be sure to read all cosmetic labels. Avoid products containing isopropyl myristrate, isopropyl palmitate, stearic acid, decylo-leate, mineral oil, lanolin and fragrance.
13. Avoid getting hair styling products on your forehead.
14. Use make-up that camouflages. Apply oil-free foundation with cover cream; with a tiny make-up brush dab away imperfections. Last, pat

lightly with translucent powder to set.
15. A surprising blemish fighter is SEX.
16. Don't worship the sun. It's a myth that the sun dries zits. It actually damages follicles which makes the break out worse. Women of all colors should use sun blocks that contain titanium dioxide or oil-free ones.
17. Do not apply perfumes, fragrances or colognes to your face to prevent irritating effects.
18. If you drive a convertible be sure to apply sun block on hot summer days.
19. Make it a habit to always wear a moisturized sun screen when out doors, winter and summer. The sun's rays can burn you even if the air feels cool, and sunlight reflected off water or the whiteness of snow can be particularly powerful.
20. No matter what your skin type is, use a high protection lotion the first time you are in the sun and don't expose your skin for more than fifteen minutes. Use a total sun screen on your face and the back of your hands, because these are constantly exposed to the sun's rays.
21. Always remove your make-up before going to bed.
22. If you usually wear make-up, give your skin a chance to breath one day a week by going without.
23. Use a humidifier to lessen the drying effects of indoor heat on your skin in the winter.
24. Take baths in the evening to avoid exposing your skin immediately to the outdoor air.

Spcial Note: Even darker skin complexions can get skin cancer, don't exempt yourself from sun block because of your race.

LIPS

~Always protect your lips with a thin coating of colorless lip balm whenever you aren't wearing lip gloss or lip color.
~For a long-lasting lipstick, apply a generous coat, then let it set for about two minutes. Blot with a tissue, puff on some powder, and then apply another generous coat of lipstick. Wait again and blot.
~Choose warm, tawny lip colors for office light.
~To make full lips appear slimmer, draw a lip line inside your natural lips line and fill with a darker shade of lip color.
~To make thin lips appear fuller, draw a lip line outside your natural lip line and

fill with a lighter shade of lipstick.

~If your upper and lower lips are uneven, apply make-up foundation over your lips, then fashion a new lip line with a pencil a shade darker than your lip color.

FOUNDATION AND BLUSH

~Test the color of foundation by applying a drop to your face or neck, rather than the back of your hand. If possible, check the color in natural light by a door or window rather than under flourescent lights in the store.

~In the winter, use oil-based, rather than water-based, make-up to protect your skin against dry, cold air.

~In the summer switch, switch to a water based foundation to help moisturize your skin, but use waterproof make-up for lips, eyes, and lashes to prevent running and smearing in the heat.

~To apply foundation evenly, use a damp sea sponge, which allows the color to blend evenly and gives the most natural-looking coverage.

~To emphasize facial contours, select a foundation that's a shade lighter than your tan.

~Use a large make-up brush to dust translucent powder lightly over your face after you've applied make-up Then further set the make-up with a light spray of mineral or ordinary water.

~To help your foundation lasts longer and give better coverage, mix it with an equal amount of skin freshner.

~To help camouflage a double chin, apply blush under the chin, then blend it upward to the bone and across toward the outer edges of the jaw.

Chapter 14

BODY BALANCE: TM

<u>DIET</u> <u>AND</u> <u>TONING</u>

Most women believe that their attitudes about food are in constant conflict with their desire to be slimmer. Trying to balance a quality exercise program in this hectic society can create road blocks for women who work, cook, clean and nurture their families around the clock. Balancing an exercise program has a multitude of benefits for women of all ages. To be at your best physically, mentally and emotionally as well as sexually, women must start by getting a complete physical evaluation. Working out with aerobics on a constant basis will help to increase your stamina and add strength. However, aerobic exercise alone, does not provide a balanced fitness program. If you expect your lover to like what he sees, then you need to get off your fanny waiting on a miracle to come to you. As you work out with aerobic and began to slim down, strength training will naturally help you to preserve lean body mass while you lose weight.

Getting plenty of exercise will help your glands work toward being in tip top shape. The major cause of weight problems lies within the foods that woman tend to eat. Problems can come from your lifestyle, professional life, daily scheduled eating time, and the intake of your foods. None of us can ignore food easily. Start paying closer attention to what you take in your body and you will began to lose weight in a healthy way. You will notice that the weight will stay off and not resurface after a few months.

Most people don't realize that they don't have to diet they just need to reduce their intake of certain foods. Eliminating that extra slice of pie or that ice cream cone on the way to bed can reduce your fat cell increase.

NUTRITION

Keep a food diary for one week (seven days). Write down everything that you put into your mouth. EVERYTHING! Even the cigarettes that you smoke should be entered into your weekly diary. Include snacks no matter how small. If you chew a piece of bubble gum write it down. It will be a little uncomfortable at first, but keeping an accurate record will only help you to become the woman that you want to be with the body that you so deserve. Have a dietitian evaluate your diary at the end of the week (don't be shy or embarrassed). A dietitian will be able to tell you which foods are high in fat content or if your portions are too much for your body to burn off effectively. Eating out can often be the source of too many wrong foods. Cook a special meal for your man at home. He'll enjoy the treat. Since you'll be watching your intake you'll be more careful of what you eat.

Restaurant foods often contain hidden fats and oils and portions are usually larger than those prepared at home. Remember that larger portions make larger bodies. Plan your menu and calorie intake and then stick to it. By having to plan your meal ahead of time, they will be balanced and nutritional and you will get the most food for your calories.

EATING PLAN

Some nutritionist and dietitians feel that your eating plan should initially start with 1200 calories daily. After feeling dizzy and suffering headaches for a day, I realized that my calorie intake was too low. Experimenting with different calorie amounts will allow you to see how many calories you should eat in order to lose weight or maintain your present weight, or even to gain weight.

Each person's metabolism is different, and each individual needs to monitor her own body to see how many calories can be consumed. Becoming a conscientious woman will be your goal. Here is most basic formula to use when trying to figure out how many calories you can eat and still lose the weight that you desire to lose. If you want to gain weight, add to what you are already intaking by calories and your job will be easier.

*estimate the number of calories needed per day for weight maintenance (based on sedentary lifestyle) by multiplying your weight in pounds by 10. Example: 140 X 10 = 1400.

*for safe weight loss of approximately one pound per week subtract 250. Example: 1400 - 250 = 1150.

If you exercise, make sure to factor in the number of calories you burn during your workout. You will only have to cut 50 calories out of your diet, rather than 250, in order to lose a half pound per week.

Avocados and nuts have a high percentage of fats. Notice the labels on everything that you eat. You might still be able to eat your favorite foods if you just monitor what you eat on a regular daily basis. Watch out for sugar free products, this ONLY means that they are free of sucrose, not of the many other types of sweeteners that are no better for you nutritionally (honey, corn, syrup). Look for foods that are enriched, fortified, low-sodium, or have added fiber.

In products with nutrition labels, make sure to check out the grams of fat per serving. Only thirty percent of your total caloric intake per day should come from dietary fats (for people who are trying to lose weight, their daily intake should be less). If you consume 1200 calories a day, only 360 of those should be from fat.

There is no need to give up your joy for food. Here are some tips to enjoy your meals without jeopardizing your calorie limit.

~set a realistic limit, remembering to nutritionally balance your menu. (Don't just order salad and then top it by ordering a dessert).

~incorporate an appetizer or bread or both into your calorie count so you're not famished by the time the meal comes.

~before ordering an entree' consider how it is prepared. You'll save a lot of calories if it's broiled or grilled dry with sauce on the side.

~Any leftover calories can be applied toward dessert or alcohol. Neither are forbidden; just plan for the calories that are your limit.

CHANGING BEHAVIORS

Some people think that food represents festivity and comfort, but like others you might turn to food when life isn't fun. Food is considered a quick fix to make people feel better. Sometimes it does so for only a short while. After indulging, people feel worse about themselves. Work on recognizing times when you're vulnerable to overeating or simply snacking out of depression or anxiety. Use alternatives like calling a friend, going for a walk or being around other people, and don't forget the most important alternative of all:

Keep a food diary. Record your mood along with what and how much you eat. Usually when a person is tired, too busy or bored, the result is overeating. When you feel like snacking, eat healthy snacks. Instead of chocolates, chips, or candy select fruits, vegetables, whole wheat pretzels or frozen diet desserts.

Learning to eat the correct foods is just like learning to play an instrument. It takes a lot of practice. You'll slip up from time to time, but the important thing is to get back in touch with your goals and never give up on improving yourself.

BODY METABOLISM MATTERS

As many of us suspected, higher metabolism is born with some people. You can boost your metabolism if you don't give up. Exercises using your leg muscles can increase your metabolism the most. Aerobics, such as running, walking, stair climbing and bicycling fires metabolism up. Strength training can also speed up your metabolism permanently because lean muscle tissue burns calories faster than fatty tissue. Increasing muscle mass takes months of work. But be patient and don't give up, because you'll enjoy as well as appreciate the end results.

The best weight loss plan is to cut calories only moderately, but you must be more active. If your activities have slowed down because of laziness but you say it's due to age, become more active to drop those unhealthy pounds. Start at a beginners pace if you haven't exercised for a long time. Then you can gradually build up your endurance to do more sets as well as repetitions.

WALKING TO HELP METABOLISM

Walking burns calories, tones muscles, strengthens bones and costs less than the price of a pair of sneakers made for walking. Walking can be taken up at any age or fitness level.

There is always something that can be said about walking. Thinking to put one foot in front of the other should sum it up, but not so. You don't even have to have sweat pouring down your face to enjoy the benefits of walking. You help your heart by walking because as you walk faster, your heart beats faster. That in turn helps to tone your heart muscle causing better efficiency in pumping blood. You will function with less fatigue and your energy level increases. It also helps to lower your chances of acquiring heart disease when you exercise. Many people believe that walking increases your appetite but it really doesn't. It increases your metabolism as it curbs your appetite.

TENSION RELIEF: WITH WALKING

Walking also firms and strengthens your calves, thighs. ankles, feet, stomach, hips and buttocks. The strong arm swing during walking helps you to maintain balance; proper stride will tone and strengthen your shoulders, upper back, chest and arm muscles. Walking can also help ease your feelings of tension and anxiety. Walking also has a continuous tranquilizing effect.

Be sure to stretch your muscles before walking to avoid strain. Toward the end of your walk gradually slow down so that your muscles have a chance to cool down. Don't go full speed and then come to a complete stop. This is not good for any part of your body.

WALKING IN WATER

To burn up to 500 calories per hour, just wade in a nearby pool, lake or beach. You won't even have to get your hair wet during warmer months. Remember to apply sun block. Walking in water as a part of your exercise program is great for losing those unwanted inches that you find difficult to loose.

Water helps to support you as you walk burning calories at a brisk rate without putting undo strain on your joints. You can begin walking in water that is only knee deep and of cool temperatures. Warm water will drive the heart rate too high so be careful. Move backward, forward, sideways, with lengthy strides. Work a bit harder with waist high water trying to maintain a twenty-minute workout of walking. Walking with your arms in the water will burn even more calories and provides a more complete workout.

A good tip to remember is if you are tired of pulling and tugging as you try to put your swimsuit on, the water workout will give you more incentive to work those pounds off. At least if you exercise in the water your flab won't be seen and you can burn off inches and calories at the same time.

OTHER WONDERS OF WATER

Many women know that water works wonders. Even though the statement is clear cut the message in the statement is sometimes confusing. We tend to take the benefits of water for granted. Of course we splash, swim, bathe, paddle, shower, and even drink it, but we need to check out some of the marvelous facts of our most prized natural resource.

DRINK PLENTY OF LIQUIDS

Water is about seventy percent of your physical being. Water helps you digest your food, and it carries the nutrients in your body. It keeps your joints lubricated and it helps to carry waste from your body. Surviving without food is possible for many weeks, but without water you wouldn't survive more than a few days. Water constantly flowing throughout your body assures your life. As we grow older, water is very necessary to keep the fluids flowing to help discard waste and to keep sending nutrients. Water aids in keeping skin moisturized as well. Keeping hydrated will assure comfortable body mechanisms that are sometimes slowed down with age.

BOTTLED WATER

Some water that has been considered filtered and chlorinated, isn't as good as bottled water. There are many brands on the market and the 1.6 billion gallons of bottled water that's consumed by Americans boils down to at least eight gallons per capita. With all the varieties there are, you are sure to find one that you like. If you have questions about your local reservoir, call your city's and or county's water company.

Here's a list of the types of bottled water:
Spring Water: sources are from natural underground.
Sparkling Water: has natural and added carbonation.
Seltzer: filtered and sodium free; during the bottled process it's carbonated.
Club Soda: filtered and carbonated; mineral salts and minerals added for taste. This one has a higher sodium count.

Mineral Water: ground water with minerals added; composition of this one varies.

Bulk Water: Purified, distilled, deionized; calcium or magnesium salts added for taste. Sold in one gallon jugs.

WET AND WATERY LETTUCE

A technique used in agriculture substitutes a solution of water and chemical fertilizers for soil. HYDROPONICS has been around since WWII. These vegetables are bland and a little watery and the advantages of year round availability is great. I've had several women to tell me that they place pieces of watery lettuce like little patches over there eyes to reduce early morning swelling of their eyes.

SPLASH TECHNIQUES

Aqua-aerobics, is the latest craze for women at health clubs. Just like water walking, try water jogging as a natural part of your aerobics workout. The advantage is there is no stress involved in splash techniques. This is great even in as little as one foot of water. I'm presently creating a book with a workout program for water aerobics. Look for it to be released soon.

When I was younger, as a part of my gymnastics workout my coach would have us to jog in tubs of water. It worked the hell out of our legs and it increased our cardiovascular endurance levels. It was GREAT.

Schedule quiet time for brainstorming

Chapter 15

MAKING TIME FOR YOU:

<u>SOLITUDE</u>

Studies are showing that women are seeking ways to relax: Guess what, one of the best ways to relax is to spend time alone. Getting away from the human race can be personally stimulating and rewarding.

Many women have found time to escape without losing compassion for their families. Solitude has rich possibilities for inner peace and personal development. Setting aside time to listen to yourself allows you the time to see the world around you more clearly. Even though good conversation is also stimulating, remaining quiet for hours at a time has wonderful benefits. Effectively incorporating solitude into your life helps you to relish and value life. By observing silent times when you don't speak, don't answer the telephone, read newspapers television or listen to the radio, you can listen to yourself instead.

If you maintain silence for a day or a major part of the day, you will experience the phenomenon of solitude. Some of the best times to solve problems are through silent times. Asking yourself pertinent questions during silent times will give clarity which in turn will give answers.

Silence should be programmed into the lives of women. Women tend to appreciate the input from their surroundings by drawing on their personal energy. Traditions of silence are ancient, and full of spiritual enlightenment. Silence is known as the "holy uselessness", a cleansing of interfering vision. Even though the dictionary describes silence as passive, absence of speech or noise, many philosophers consider it active and complex.

Silence is the voice of the soul. When you're talking or preparing to talk, you are deaf to songs within. A calmer mind is reflected during silence. Creativity flourishes as it provides a chance to grow from thoughts within. Silence can also free negative energies. Finding a time to experience solitude will help to give thoughts, ideas and creativity to yourself. Psychiatrist Anthony Storer, M.D., author of <u>Solitude: A Return to the Self,</u> explains how a woman wrote him to tell how she escaped to her bedroom each afternoon, not because she needed sleep, but because she had to be alert to the needs of others without regards to her own needs.

Listening to yourself helps you realize how much you really do or don't know. It helps to reduce the expenditure of excessive energy. Intimate silence can bring peak moments to your life.

<u>VALUABLE</u> <u>USES</u> <u>OF</u> <u>SILENCE</u>

Some other valuable uses of silence are that it:
-provides time for continued success,
-provides opportunity to explore thoughts,
-allows times for completing thoughts,
-allows sensitive feelings of physical presence,

Silence creates a sanctuary of self observation. Many people distrusts silence because society discourages it, therefore it is feared. Since quietness is seen as rejection or fear, it is not easy to recognize as the inner voice of strength. Some people call it arrogance, while others see it as a form of sadness. Silence has been smothered in today's busy and noisy world of information. Reviving the values of silence are now being done at retreats, and religious centers so that the minds can be nourished by tranquillity. Retreats can sometimes provide spiritual renewal. Silence releases the power to express yourself. Women are seeking contemplation in our society, and finding out that they don't have to leave home to obtain its benefits is great.

Silence can be discovered in your everyday life. Creating an environment to succeed with silent commitment is necessary to capture it's true benefits. Here are some basic guidelines to follow:

BASIC GUIDELINES TO FOLLOW:

1. **Have the person or people with whom you live to actively cooperate.**
   Cooperation is crucial to your growth in silence. Silence can sometimes feel like rejection to your loved ones, so explain why silent times are so important to you. Using these times as enclosed curtains for yourself instead of a door to shut out loved ones will help to create the support needed from your family.

2. **Share your silence.**
   Being quiet together can add new life to your relationship. It's okay to smile, to touch and to look into each others eyes from time to time with nonverbal communication.

3. **Bring your children into your circle of silence.**
   Encourage them to bring silent times into their own lives. It helps them to value the ability to concentrate as well as make graceful exits from arguments. It enables them to release stress by learning to calm themselves.

4. **Schedule silent times.**
   Set aside time in your day for being completely silent. You can choose the time of day as well as the amount of time you'll use. You're making time for you so you can make the rules. Remember that once you make the rules it will be easier to stick to them.

5. **Explain silent times.**
   It's your decision whether or not you explain your personal solitude. People are going to form their own opinions regardless of the true reason why, so why not be unavailable during these times. After all isn't that the purpose of silent times?

6. **Ways to spend time during solitude.**
   -enjoy a long quiet ride alone in your car.
   -take a walk in the early morning dawn.

-take a walk in the quiet evening dusk.
-take a quiet walk along the beach.
-suggest a silent bike ride with your lover.
-encourage a quiet hike.
-sit on top of a hill to recapture the essence of nature.
-enclose yourself in your favorite room in your home and lavish
  solitude upon yourself.

You may want to do something different each time you reward your self with silence. You may choose to quietly cook, clean, garden, write poems or short stories. A quiet place offers creativity. Doing nothing at all is also nice for nourishing your soul.

7. <u>Make use of the tools available to you.</u>

When out in public, wearing headphones without playing anything keeps people from distracting you or talking to you. Use your answering machine to intercept your telephone calls while integrating silent times at home. Silence is new to many women, so exploration is different. The wonderful impacts that solitude is having on my life is beneficial in the ways that I spend my days. It helps to awaken my consciousness. Solitude strengthens my senses to the natural world around me. When a bird chirps or the wind whistles I notice. I realized that I don't have to be active all the time, because I am content with being quietly me. Short sessions of solitude are appreciated because stillness is now a valuable opportunity to cherish me. I value and cherish times that I can be at peace with myself. Capturing the world of silence is an intimate relationship with ones-self.

Chapter 16

DOUCHING AND CLEANSING:

CLEANSING THE VAGINA

Women should be very selective as to whether they should cleanse the vagina and/or the anus. Both openings have their own special odors and body fragrances. Every woman's body is unique and odors uniquely different. No two smell the same. Just as finger prints are different, so are body odors. This odor varies due to many reasons. Many things are a common factor in body odors so before you began to douche excessively, get in tune with your body to find out why you possess these odors.

Some common reasons for odors:
1. Diet and eating habits
2. Medications
3. Exercise program
4. Rest factor
5. Body oils and perfumes

6. Lotions
7. Powders
8. Water source
9. Soap or cleansing product
10. Skin type or condition of skin
11. Body functions
12. Frequency of sex
13. Masturbation habits and fluids
14. Vaginal secretions
15. Menstrual cycle

Douching is not necessary to cleanse the vagina. The normal, healthy vagina naturally cleans itself. If you feel it personally necessary to douche after your period, you can do so with little worry of developing problems. Women who douche too frequently, however, can destroy the colonies of beneficial bacteria that normally inhabit the vagina, leaving it vulnerable to organisms that cause vaginitis (inflammation of the vagina). Most women douche when they smell unpleasant odors or experience excessive discharges. But the vagina will not have a continuous bad odor unless an infection exists so if you notice an unusual smell or discharge that you can't seem to combat, rather than trying to douche it away, see your doctor.

Good, personal feminine hygiene makes oral sex more attractive, but you don't need to douche in preparation for oral sex. Simply wash the external vaginal area carefully. A dash of perfumes or fragrances on your inner thighs or your panty line will add sensual allure for your partner. I recommend a perfume that's light and pleasant, not too spicy or too strong. You don't want your lover to love the smell and hate the taste because you've over did the perfume.

CLEANSING THE CLITORIS

The clitoris is hardly ever mentioned when we talk about cleaning the sex organs, but it needs proper cleaning also. Located at the head of the vagina, covered by fluffy skin under the labia it stands to be dealt with in more ways than one. It is often called the love button due to its sensitive nature in helping women to achieve orgasms. As you pull the skin of the labia back, gently take a cotton swab and with circular motions swab gently until the white mucous that is embedded there is eliminated. Don't try to clean it too well because the natural secretions of this orifice are healthy. You would only want to cleanse it after love-making or your monthly period has ended. Sometimes the fluids from sex and period trash will hide inside the skin folds of your love button causing undo odors that are rarely detected and never cleaned. Bacteria and unwanted odors in this area are difficult to detect because we never look for them here.

CLEANSING THE ANUS

The anus should be cleaned just as any other part of your body should be cleaned. Washed carefully to rid it of all excrement and bacteria that settles after a bowel movement. Wiping with tissue after having a bowel movement is not enough to say that it is thoroughly cleaned. Time and care should be given to cleaning it well.

With the constant streaks, skid marks, or mud marks, (as women call them), showing up on a regular basis in our son's, husband's, or boyfriend's underwear, we as women should began to wonder just how clean our men are. Women have personal accessories that are included within their douche packets that can be used to clean the anus, but our men are left to dig, pull, wipe and scuff endlessly only to share their skid marks with the rest of the wash. The anus should be wiped and cleaned thoroughly, after each bowel movement. One of the best ways suggested by women to clean the anus is to wipe from front to back several times after a bowel movement. Cup the toilet tissue and wipe again, even if you think you've cleaned all residue, wipe one more time for practical measures. You'll use more tissue than normal, but it's worth it to feel clean. I've gone to great lengths to find the answer to an obvious, but well kept secret. "Why do men have bowel streaks in their underwear on a regular basis"? My theory is that the amount of times that men actually sit down to use the commode is less than women by far. Therefore, women wipe their anus more often than men. You see the fact is men stand while urinating, women sit, therefore women wiped fifty percent more than men. Whether it was wiping their vagina or their anus women still wiped more often.

Women are taught as children to wipe their vaginal sections after each use on the toilet. We are taught and trained to wipe from the front toward the back, which leads me to believe that we actually wipe our anus with almost every toilet use. Each woman that I interviewed said that almost every single time that they used the toilet they wiped their anus whether intentionally or not. It was primarily a habitual reflex. Therefore, evidence proves that men are susceptible to producing long-time streaks in their underwear far more than women.

**The most important secret for a woman to keep
is the opinion of herself.**

Chapter 17

SINGLE WOMEN

In the last half of this wonderful century, women's attitudes toward being single have changed tremendously. Many opportunities for single women are now available to allow them to lead a complete life with benefits to overcome all obstacles. In spite of the new attitudes toward single women nothing can change the initial shock when one loses a spouse or a lover through death or rejection. One's ego, always fragile, may be battered and it can be a time when self-pity flourishes to the detriment of one's energies.

The goal of most women in life is to be happy. This is even more true for the single person than for anyone else. Being a single woman should be looked upon as an opportunity for positive action and a time for special fulfillments. Hobbies and interests that have been dormant for years can be nurtured anew. Furthering your education can open doors to new experiences and new interests can be pursued, perfected and enjoyed.

Being single is a time to feel proud of oneself, a time to get one's act together. It's a time to get well organized, have an affirmative attitude and keep the eyes wide open so that one does not miss the new directions and opportunities that lie ahead.

Single woman have a responsibility to society for their actions. There are times when you will be tempted to get involved with more than one man or even a married man. You will worry about whether he is right or wrong for you. Everything that a single girl wants is not always what she needs. Every man that she wants is not always right for her either.

SINGLE WOMAN'S ETHICS

Developing ethics is very important in this day and age. My single friends have given me a set of rules that they follow:

1. Keep your hands, body, lips and mouth off your sister's or your best friend's man.
2. Don't let any man touch you or make love with you who you don't like and don't really want to have a relationship with.
3. Give yourself completely to the man you love.
4. Respect the man you love and demand respect from him.
5. Don't tease or lead a man on giving physical or emotional promises.
6. Keep the fidelity promised to one man and keep your word and stick to it.
7. Don't have sex with more men than you can physically handle.
8. Flirt all you want quietly, it not only builds your ego it also keeps you in practice.
9. Don't make flirtatious promises that you can't keep.
10. Be sexually responsive to your man.

Once you've become sensuous you will be an adored, admired and attractive woman to all men, but this does not give you permission to use this gift in a negative way. Arrive at a set of personal ethics that are morally workable. Let these ethics remain clear in your mind and do not become a heart breaker. You want to be thought of as delicious, sensuous, sexy and as an adoring WOMAN, not a user. Unpleasant situations usually accompany a person who has no sexual ethics. Take responsibility for your personal actions and your personal decisions will be easier to reach.

I believe that if you use sex as a means of making money, you will lose your sensitive edge because it turns into business only attitudes. But I also believe that a woman must do what she has to do to survive...and I know that a woman of imagination should never be without money if she uses her tools in the correct ways.

SINGLE WOMEN AFFIRMATIVES

1. **Get a job and keep a job.** For some women this the most important option of all; proper preparation should began at once. If you don't have a job this one can be the most difficult to accomplish. A single woman with a job is more positive and confident.

2. **Increase volunteer work as a single women.** This helps to etch your name into this world's history.

3. **Travel trying new places rather than the same old place**. You add more excitement and a more exploring attitude.

4. **Further your education by taking some classes or courses** that you've always wanted to take, but never got the chance to take. It's always best to increase your knowledge of the arts. This provides opportunities to meet new people. In addition it provides networking opportunities to meet business people who might be able to offer other advancements to your career objectives.

5. **Follow an intensive physical improvement plan,** which should involve your health, diet, exercise, and good looks, more exercise, new hairdo, make-over and so on.

6. **Enter into politics** by joining a local organization and become active in your community's upkeep.

7. **Read more often and keep yourself better informed** so that your conversation has an added sparkle.

8. **Seek psychological counseling if you need it.** Don't be ashamed to get it all together. Shop around for the right person who will understand your personal needs.

9. **Become an expert in something** whether its dancing, jogging or playing dominoes.

10. **Make new friends of both sexes,** with all the new ideas and facets of your life people will naturally want to be around you.

11. **Rediscover your hidden talents in the performing and creative arts**

12. **Fix up your environment at home.** If your home is badly in need of repairs or redecoration and you just can't afford it, then redesign so that your interior elements will look fresh, warm and inviting.

13. **Entertain:** Do it well, often and with imagination. If you can't afford to buy the needed items do as I do and invite people who don't mind pitching in and bringing the necessary items.

14. **Buy the pet of your choice.** A pet will provide the company that you need at all times and it will break the stillness of the home. And pets can also help you to become a more lovable person.

15. **Remember to go to church.** It's a great healer of loneliness. While in church you are a part of the greatest coming together there is, LOVE.

You can either be an admirable single woman or an crusty old maid. The choice is yours.

TM

Chapter 18

INSURANCE POLICIES

Some women never think of taking out insurance policies on their boyfriends. Entering into relationships that are lasting longer without the commitment of marriage have become common place in our culture. Women are getting to know their partners on a long-term basis before marriage enters the picture. Once a woman moves in or lets her lover move in, she should consider the insurance benefits for the both of them. You've got to remember the business aspect of all that matters. Taking care of business is important in case the relationship ends in death. No one likes the idea of taking out life insurance, but we must do what we have to do as women. Consider these important reasons for having insurance on your lover :

Reason #1
You moved in with him four years ago. Now he's dead but all the bills he had are still alive and due. Collecting his insurance benefits will help pay off his debts as well as yours. Besides he probably owes you every dime.

Reason #2

He's married. His wife probably is going to get everything of real value. So what, you don't care because you took out a separate policy on him that will get you everything that you need and want. Besides, he owes it to you for all the bull you put up with, especially those times he stood you up because she had plans that overruled yours.

Reason #3

It's the business thing to do. You were so mesmerized with him when you first met him that you had no idea he was penniless. If anything does happen to him, (God forbid), at least you'll be able to thank him for leaving you with money after death that you didn't have during his lifetime. These may not be the nicest reasons to take out insurance policies, but any woman who lives with a man should consider it wise to have insurance on him.

TYPES OF INSURANCE POLICIES

There are three types of insurance policies that I'll discuss. They are:

1. Dental and Medical Insurance
2. Disability Insurance
3. Life Insurance

Medical and dental insurance pays doctor and hospital bills and it may sometimes cover home visits, doctor office visits and hospital bills.

Disability insurance pays a monthly stipend if you are injured, ill or disabled and can't work temporarily or permanently.

Life insurance upon death pays a specified lump sum to your beneficiary. Applying for an insurance policy will present a few standard procedures. The insurance company will ask you several questions about your past and current health history. They will ask permission to obtain further information from your doctor. You will sometimes be asked to undergo a medical exam conducted by the insurance company. A consent to take blood will also include a test for HIV.

If you have a pre-existing condition, some insurance companies might not insure you. Pre-existing illness means a medical condition you suffered before your application. Virtually all insurance companies refuse to insure people who are HIV-positive, while some other companies reject people with cancer or heart disease. Still other companies require a waiting period. During this time you can not have a pre-existing illness, but after this waiting period you will be covered. Some insurance companies will not pay for experimental medicines or treatments even if it may save a person's life. Read the insurance booklet from your company to check for any pre-existing rules and regulations.

Try your best to be as honest as possible on these forms because if you don't it will be considered insurance fraud, which is against the law. If you are caught giving false information on your insurance forms you can be dropped.

Since coverage problems are a delicate subject, you need to establish a good relationship with your family doctor by taking an active part in your insurance forms. Seek a good insurance agent also, one who will discuss your insurance options thoroughly. Since some insurance companies are government regulated it is important to search out the information that you need about insurance from a professional insurance agent. Now-a-days you can find one by using your local yellow pages, word of mouth or a family member.

Should you ever need to leave work due to illness, long term or short term, the federal law protects your insurance. Say, for instance, that you leave your present job for a new job, but the new company's insurance has a waiting period of six months. You may continue your insurance with your former job until the waiting period is up. Once the waiting period is up you may then drop the old coverage and add the new. The laws are changing constantly in insurance, so be sure to talk to your local insurance agent if you have any questions concerning insurance benefits.

**Men, even if you think you understand them..
never let them know**

TM

Chapter 19

MARRIED WOMEN

The truth about marriage is that marriages are usually started with the romance that's made in heaven, but real love like real women often begins long after passion has cooled and fantasies have ended.

Let's say you are in a relationship, you feel good about yourself with this wonderful man. You see a new you, you feel good about talking to him and you like all the things that the two of you have in common. You're having fun, you feel the fire when you are with him, and you enjoy the love and intimacy with him. Just the two of you is all that's needed and you feel that you are in the middle of one of your favorite love songs.

If what I described sounds good to you, then that's the type of relationship you need to be in. But guess what usually destroys this beautiful scenario. MARRIAGE. This type of relationship on its own, left on its own will eventually die of natural causes. That's what it's suppose to do, so some people think. Making a marriage out of it will put it on a disabled list for a life time. You almost have it all, a gratifying relationship, a comfortable home, a great car and money in the bank adds to this bliss.

After the romance, marriage is the path to creation, and in between is the crossroads. As long as you can keep the stars bright, dreams flourishing, love beaming and life hopeful your marriage can and will survive.

There is no one answer to a successful marriage because at some point and time all couples have arguments or disagreements and these arguments or disagreements can sometimes get out of hand, therefore creating friction that can sometimes be unrepaired. It takes lots of hard work, determination, and dedication to remain steadfast in a marriage. When living together in matrimony whether holy or not, times can be rough if couples aren't willing to bend a little. Marriage is a give and take with many ups and downs. Each will have to give and someone will have to take a little. Those who enter into marriage should be really in love for the duration of it because without true love it is only a relationship destined to be shortened. Marriage is a journey of self-discovery. You help to discover each other and others help to discover you. People usually chart their lives by getting married, add to the foundation by having children and allow history to be made by doing something positive in their lifetime of marriage.

SENSUALITY AFTER MARRIAGE

Showing married women how to hold on to the creative energy and their sensuality is only part of the scope in this section. Most married women are not particularly unhappy in their marriages, nor are they taking their marriage vows lightly. Married women are seeking continuous excitement in their relationships from their husbands. Sometimes, however, they are finding themselves in unexpected affairs that are difficult to leave because of the much needed excitement and romance. Most women who have ventured into affairs tell me that they don't feel guilt, conflict, or remorse. Dalma Heyn, wrote the book Erotic Silence of the American Wife, which gives great reports on the wife and her erotic ventures. She states that women felt awakened and revived from their emotional numbness that had settled on them after marriage once an affair began. Many married women that I interviewed noted that they didn't even realize their height of sexuality until they had an extramarital affair. They also realized that they had misplaced their passion until a secret friendship with a dazzling man brought them to their sexual senses. They all agreed that their affair was needed to sexually physically, financially or emotionally fill a void. Most women who have affairs feel that their marriages improve because their tolerance levels improves. Things that normally upset them with their husbands had ceased to upset them because of their outside relationships and activities.

The desire to be sensuous had come back anew, alive and vibrantly fresh. Since their marriages had lost life, their outside relationships filled a major void. Being married has made many women feel less sexy and romantic. Their capacity for desire and pleasure in the bed was lost with their husbands. As many wives are feeling half dead, muted, stifled, frozen, and hollow due to lack of activity in their sex lives so are their husbands. These feelings are giving those once healthy marriages a bad name. Women who are married are sometimes experiencing erotic silence which is often associated with depression in housewives. Statistics show that twenty-two percent of married women are suffering from depression compared to single women. Marriage is proving to be more and more harmful to many women. Marriage for centuries has asked women to become selfless. It began with the woman dropping her birth name to take his name on a borrowed basis. I even have women tell me that when they divorced, some of the husbands, as a part of the divorce agreement, wanted their last names back. She gives up her right to carry her name just to justify his ownership. A women gives up her heritage in this respect.

Many women have learned to hide their emotions from their husbands, so as not to upset him. With her lover, she does whatever she feels at the moment and that's what brings them closer. Her husband she feels get the better her, the easier her. This is where her female sexuality as a wife dies, but as a woman sometimes begins. Many married women believe that staying alive in marriage isn't about just the sex, it's about having the freedom to be yourself sexually, without the stereotyped cultural requirements. Marriage is a welcoming of the so-called good woman, one that takes care of everyone even if that means neglecting herself, which in turn means neglecting sexual gratification and satisfaction.

More married women today than ever before, have had sex before marriage. They have several lovers, and several careers while married. The fact that women are seeking their self-fulfillment is causing people to consider women selfish and uncaring. Many married women are stagnated by the guilt that they cannot be the perfect wife, mother, homemaker, and the perfect wage earner. The prehistoric ideals of what it takes to qualify women as good wives are long gone. One of the reasons that this way of living is gone is due to the fact that it's hard to live up to it and still remain healthy.

As women try to hide their past or disregard their sexual histories and pains they suddenly began to feel ashamed. Married women are finding it healthy to admit to their husbands their sexual wants, needs and desires. The problem comes when he asks questions about her sexual past. She will sometimes feel ashamed causing her true sexual self to go in hiding.

All the rituals of becoming a new and better person are significant to many women. These rituals are about cleansing and purifying. The symbolic wedding dress represents purity, innocence and honesty. Trying to symbolize your innocence by being perfect is not healthy. After all, no one is perfect, not even the man you love or the one you will love. This is not a perfect world.

Some women go as far as to try to hide their sexuality by diminishing their sexual experiences that led to their sexual knowledge. Today women are increasingly entering their marriages with numerous sexual histories. Why some women are pretending that they have no sexual history is still a mystery. The 'still a virgin' characteristic exists in woman in order to protect their husband's ego and their reputations. Some women think that it's too bold or too unattractive to say otherwise.

Some of the phrases used to control or silence a woman in order to protect her man's vulnerability and her sexuality:

~he might disapprove

~he might refuse her sex

~he might lose his erection

~he might think she's selfish

~he might call her overbearing

~he might call her a loose woman

A woman's expectations of sex have been so limited in the past that she sometimes get a headache worrying about it. It's not the fact that she doesn't get sex, she doesn't get good sex. Some women stated that, after being married for a while, pleasure dies and so does her interest in all the marital bliss that thrilled her before the marriage. Since sex is a natural expectation of marriage, when problems arise, sex usually suffers first.

Listed in the next chapter are ways to get the home fires burning again in marriages. These warm to hot techniques are great for all couples who want to revive the sensuous aspects of their relationships.

WHY MARRIED WOMEN HAVE AFFAIRS

Women who are having affairs report several reasons for their actions. One is that the communication between she and her husband is limited or sometimes to the point of nonexistence. I am not telling women to have affairs, but I will tell women who are married, "why not try to have an affair with your husband". In order to get your sexuality back, (and if your relationship has any hope of surviving) you must began anew with sensuality. I'm not advocating affairs, but you have to wonder what makes a woman get to this point. An affair is complicated and it's complications can easily turn a marriage into a divorce. Second, pleasure is lacking and often missing from long time marriages. Women are not afraid to say that they need pleasure. And what they feel in affairs is passion. The third reason women are having affairs is that an affair is healing to them. It makes her feel free to make choices that she wouldn't otherwise make. She feels free to be herself, and in turn she begins to love herself again. She also finds her lost sexual self. The last reason is she's glad to find a friend who she can be her honest and true self with. An affair allows her to share her secrets with someone who won't judge or put her down.

Affairs have been noted as being truthful as difficult as this may seem, affairs derive from being able to tell the truth. In an affair, a woman can be herself. She's not afraid to be honest with her lover so she releases some undue tension that would otherwise be bottled inside of her. Women felt comfortable in an affair, because they didn't experience sexual inhibitions. The women who I talked with said that the only thing that they regretted about having an affair is the lying. They felt ashamed for lying to their husbands, especially if the husbands hadn't did anything to hurt her. All in all women were glad that they had affairs.

The best way to break the cycle of affairs is to stay in tune with what your husband likes sexually and tell him what you like sexually. If you feel that the sexuality in your marriage is slipping get to know each other again. Try not to give up on your relationship. Make an effort to show your husband your real sexual self. Once he experiences the real you, not his ideal of you, your sexuality and yourself will cease to be at risk.

When a woman is silent sexually, she loses her sexuality. This in turn limits her pleasure, therefore poisoning her whole sexual self. Female self-sacrifice is a matter of choice based on family values and morality codes. Excluding your needs leads to a dissatisfied woman. If the woman is unhappy, the family is usually unhappy. Let your family know that your pleasures of life, fulfillment and happiness are important to you. Let them know that you have a life too. Your children should be raised to know that even though you are their mother, you have a life too. Go out and dance once in a while. Go to the movies without the children sometimes. Being married does not mean that you lose you, or your identity as a person. Helping your children to understand that you are pleasure-loving person will help them to accept women as people who are caring and fulfilled.

Chapter 20

AWAKENING SEXUAL SENSES:

WARM TO HOT

While gently teasing your man you can strike an erogenous zone. Lightly massage the inside of his arms and his palms: gently massage the inside of his thighs as you knead them. Run your fingers over other parts of his body that you consider just as erogenous. The good thing about this type of awakening is that you can do it with your clothes on, or off. You can also do these things as you snuggle in front of the television, a lit fireplace or even while passing one another in the living room.

*While hugging him give him a teasingly slow rotation of your pelvic bone against his groin.

*Massage the back of his neck.

*Stroke his body parts that you most like.

*Make an erotic telephone call or leave a love note for him in his lunch or briefcase.

*Take full advantage of all erections.

*Wrestle naked playfully as you catch him stepping out of the tub or shower.
*Greet him at the door naked.
*Put on some mellow music and get him away from the TV so you can dance slowly and erotic.
*Take a bath together.
*Take a shower together in a darkened room.
*Tell him that you love to look and touch his naked body.
*Purchase him a pair of satin boxers.
*Read WILL THE REAL WOMEN PLEASE STAND UP to him as erotically as you can.
* Give each other foot massages, and relaxing back rubs.
*Kiss each other passionately everytime you kiss.

PHASE ONE: SENSITIVITY

Let's begin this phase by doing something very simple. To test your sensitivity, go to a secluded spot of your choice...it can be your car, your lounge, or your bed. It doesn't matter where, as long as you're alone. Close your eyes and let your body go limp. Think of long hard objects only. Frozen link sausages, chicken legs, empty bottles, cucumbers, carrots, dildo or even a long erect and hard penis. I hope that I've helped to awaken your senses by now.

Memorize your favorite objects. The size shape, length, width and texture. Think of all the unexpected qualities like the smoothness of each. Compare the differences, the likes and dislikes. You'll be amazed and sometimes excited about your memory.

For a week practice on your memory skills this way to increase your sensitive awareness of shapes, sizes and textures. This improves your sensitivity toward your sexual partner. Another good thing that you can do is to change the items on each day and discover how the objects come to life in your hands as you touch, feel, and caress them with your eyes closed. Bring out your sensitive side with each touch.   Get mentally lost in the feelings of each object.

PHASE TWO: AWARENESS

In this sexual awareness phase, you'll memorize the items in phase one that you got to know. Manipulate your mind, arouse your sexual appetite and automatically feel the heat. If you practiced the phase one sensory tactics as suggested, you should feel a tingle or goose bumps as you think of the objects.

To help you, think of your favorite long, hard and sensuous objects slowly sliding inside you. Imagine the depth of it all as it eases out under the control of you and no one else. Don't be shy or inhibited. You've got to get past the idea of it all in order to grasp the technique fully. I promise you once you can imagine the eroticism of it, you will feel the tingle of it. To help you to coast into this pleasure center of your brain...imagine you gripping your lover's long, hard, erect penis between your hands, your breasts, down your stomach and slowly sliding against your clitoris and finally inside your wet vagina. As your vagina dampens with anticipation you'll feel a tingle of pleasure. Ummmmmmmm, imagine these pleasures as you tingle your way to sensuality.

PHASE THREE: MOISTURIZE

This phase is the most important phase that you should do each night before falling asleep. Run a warm bath and add your favorite bath oil, cologne, or fragrance. As your water is filling the tub, rub your body with your favorite moisturizer and scan your favorite book, Will The Real Women Please Stand Up. Unwind and let your senses lock in. Play your favorite jazz selection and cut all the lights off.

Tell everyone that lives with you that you would like some privacy and relaxation. Light a small scented candle and sit in your freshly filled tub of water. Relax completely; this includes physically and mentally. Guide your mood and enhance your senses by thinking of nothing but relaxation and pleasures of sensuality. Let your quiet surroundings swallow you up as the scents entice you. Let the light from the candle dance in your mind as it flickers you into an intensely mellow mood. Allow the water to envelope your sensitive body. Let the mood romance your every needed desire as you humble your soul to the pleasures of it all. Pull a hand full of water toward you and feel the water as it trickles down your chest, between your breast and across your neck. Close your eyes now and listen to your soft playing music as you gather your senses of all the peacefulness around you. Imagine the water as it surrounds your entire body. Discover the smoothness of the water as it ripples to your every movement. Grasp mental pictures of the water and your body sitting in it. Lose yourself in your thoughts and when you began to feel drowsy, remove your new self from your tub. Included in the next section are sensuous beauty baths that will enable you to become a more seductive woman.

PHASE FOUR: ENJOYING YOU

Each person's body is unique. In this phase of sensuality, you will be able to enjoy your own body. This enables you to reach maximum pleasures in love-making. No matter what frame your body is you are special. Take time to discover you. Have pride in you, as well as your body. Take your towel and dry off very slowly. With every stroke of your towel blot yourself gently as if you are drying off a newborn baby's bottom. Apply your favorite body lotion to your entire body. To help improve your senses, rub your favorite lotion on your body with your eyes closed. Try to get to know your body as you incorporate this sensuality phase. Know where every hump, bump and mole is on your body. Begin a whole new friendship with your body. After all, you are getting to know you.

Once you've blotted any remaining lotion off of yourself, pull your bed covers back and ease into your bed naked. Sensuously sexy is how you should feel. You should fall asleep almost instantly. Sweet dreams. Don't forget to blow out remaining candles before preparing for a good nights sleep.

PHASE FIVE: SENSUOUS BATHS

Phase five consist of several types of beauty baths that can be used as a sensual stimulation toward other fulfilling moments. Your mind, body and love life will all benefits from these baths.

1. APHRODISIAC:
Turn your tub into foreplay, invite him to join you in a bath spiked with two to three tablespoons of grated gingeroot, fresh mint leaves and cinnamon. For an added arousing effect, feast on champagne and your favorite appetizers.

2. SLEEP INDUCER:
Soak in tea instead of drinking it before going to bed. Steep four bags each of tangerine lavender and chamomile tea in a pot of boiling water. Add this mixture to your bath and submerge yourself in the tub. Close the room up to seal in the steamed aroma. Relax for ten minutes or more as you inhale the scents. You'll be able to fall asleep sooner after the sleep inducer bath.

3. AT HOME SALT GLOW:
Prepare a grainy mixture of two cups of epsom salt and one cup of baby oil. Set the mixture aside as you soak in plain warm water from ten to fifteen minutes, then stand up and rub concoction into legs, arms, belly, back and buttocks. Rinse in the shower , dry off skin and smooth on more baby oil.

4. AFTER SPORTS MUSCLE RELAXER:

After a good work out to ease muscle spasms or tightness, spice warm tub with a teaspoon of dry mustard, thyme, and lavender. Soak for ten to fifteen minutes. Don't forget to:

~ soak no longer than twenty minutes, to prevent dehydrating;

~ best water temperature is 85 degrees;

~use a pumice stone on feet, and loafah on knees, elbows, bikini line
   you'll feel like silk and he'll love touching you;

~moisturize immediately after bathing. It seals in water that your skin
   has absorbed taking years off of aging skin;

~light the candles around the tub while playing your favorite
   soft music.

Lavish care on yourself. Enjoy yourself to the fullest. Forget all the negatives and lift up your spirits. Began to think good thoughts about yourself, and enjoy, enjoy, enjoy. Remember that cold water baths are refreshing; warm water baths are soothing;   hot water baths are relaxing.

5. CHAMPAGNE BATH:

This is more erotic when bathing with your lover. Bring a chilled bottle of champagne to your hot tub or bath. As you bathe sip the champagne slowly. Be sure to finish the bottle in thirty to forty minutes. During that time dream up the most sensuous thing that you're going to do to your lover. Just talking and laughing adds to the pleasures of the champagne bath. Pouring small trickles down his back or on his chest while bathing is quite refreshing.

Have a Sunday kind of love.

Chapter 21

SEXUALITY

Okay let's dive right in. A woman spends a great deal of her days and nights being aware of her sexuality. She moistens and throbs on some occasions involuntarily. As a result of all she has learned from other women and friends her age, she is impressed that her sex is a bonafide point of leverage that can be used to get her way with men.

A woman uses her sexuality to entice men and will often present the intensity of her sexual desire to get his attention. A real woman lays sexual bait for her prey and will behave seductively when she is alone with a man she is trying to lure.

Women adore men, and getting them into bed is part of the fun. Once a woman sets out to get a man, she goes all out to bait him in. Of course, the spark of it all is to succeed in getting the prize (him). Some men feel that a women will try to lure him into bed so that they will have certain rights in his life. This is not necessarily true. Women connect sex and love. When a woman gives the ultimate to her man, meaning her body, she has given her heart as well. A measure of this sex and love or at least romance shows that love is thought of as a part of bonding.

Women are romantic creatures and in the presence of men their confidence will be either sky high or very low. In this section I will focus on the higher levels of sexual self-esteem and your sexual appetite.

A true sensuous woman, with a healthy sexual appetite:

~allows an open line of communication because she is a romantic creature.
~should always feel beautiful and desirable.
~does not believe everything that a man tells her.
~should accept compliments honestly with direct eye contact to the giver of the compliment, smile and give a cordial thank you.
~should be able to accept phone calls, compliments, and flowers without feeling an obligation to have sex.
~enjoys the attention that a man gives her, but doesn't take advantage of his kindness or generosities.
~doesn't give too much or too little of herself.
~gives body language signals that send messages of sex and romance only to someone she is honestly interested in.
~will get to know her sexual partner.
~will learn to trust her man.
~will believe in him.
~will be very selective about her sexual partner.
~won't make it a habit of blaming or accusing.
~won't sleep and tell.
~won't be pretentious during sex.
~will tell him what feels good.
~will tell him what feels painful.
~will be open, honest and friendly.
~won't expect him to figure out what she enjoys sexually, she'll let him know.
~won't use sex as a weapon against him, by denying it to him.
~won't use sex as a manipulative measure to get things.
~won't use her vagina and body as an aspect of being that which gives existence and value.
~will promote herself in a positive way without sex.
~will be able to touch, caress, stroke and give lots of hugging daily to her partner.
~will respect her lover.

~will respect herself.
~will try her best not to settle for less in any form or fashion.
~tries to pick times that will accommodate both of you, such as times that you
  know he's feeling positive or after a success or good news.
~will remain playful and cuddle often.
~will show that she values him when she's not involved in genital sex.
~will make positive sexual overtures often
~will be creative and won't get angry just because he lacks sexual desire.
Remember that love travels fast, "sensuality outlives love."

SEXUAL SELF-ESTEEM

What really is sexual self-esteem? Experts and their thousands of studies can't seem to agree on what sexual self-esteem is or how to measure it precisely. Many experts do agree that self-esteem is associated with being satisfied with one's self, having confidence and pride in one's self.

Naturally, women who were brought up to be modest about their talents and strengths might be less egotistical. For years men, not women, have been reported to have higher self-esteem. Most self-esteem tests rate men higher than women. Women are now increasing their levels of sexual self-esteem by reading books like WILL THE REAL WOMEN PLEASE STAND UP and they are beginning to become increasingly satisfied with themselves. Therefore creating a " go-for-it" attitude defines a healthy level of self-esteem.

Using the standard method, your sexual self-esteem can be calculated. Answer the following questions to calculate your sexual self-esteem.

1. I take a positive attitude toward myself.
   a. strongly disagree=5
   b. disagree=4
   c. agree=3
   d. strongly agree=2

2. How often do you have sex?
   a. everyday=1
   b. 2 to 3 times a week=2
   c. about once a month=3
   d. one or two times a month=4
   e. about 6 times a year=5

3. At times I think I am no good at all.
   a. strongly disagree=5
   b. disagree=4
   c. strongly agree=3
   d. agree=2

4. Rate your sex life.
   a. poor=1   b. fair=2
   c. good=3   d. very good=4
   e. excellent=5

5. On the whole I am satisfied with myself.
    a. strongly disagree=5
    b. disagree=4
    c. strongly agree=3
    d. agree=2

6. How often do you masturbate?
    a. once a day=1
    b. 3 to 5 times a week=2
    c. 2 to 3 times a month=3
    d. 3 to 5 times a year=4

7. Often, I really feel disgusted with myself.
    a. strongly disagree=1
    b. disagree=2
    c. agree=3
    d. strongly agree=4

8. Has your partner performed oral sex on you?
    a. yes, often=1
    b. yes, seldom=2
    c. yes, rarely
    d. no=4

9. I first had sexual intercourse when I was
    a. 10 - 15 years old=1
    b. 16-21 years old=2
    c. 21-26 years old=3
    d. never been sexually active =5

10. How many orgasms do you have in one lovemaking session?
    a. none=1   b. one=2
    c. two or more=3

11. How many sexual partners have you had first sexual encounter?
    a. on to three=1
    b. four to six=2
    c. seven to ten=3
    d. eleven to twenty=4

12. What is your marital status?

    a. single, living alone=1
    b. single, living with parent=2
    c. married=3
    d. seperated=4
    e. divorced=5
    f. widowed=6

Add the numbers corresponding to your answers. If the total is eight or less you have a low self esteem. If the median is ten or more you have a high self-esteem.

The percentage of women who score high on self-esteem are presently thirty-four percent. Women who score medium on self esteem are 21% and women who score low on self esteem are forty-five percent. These percentages are increasingly higher than five years ago.

If experts defined sexual self-esteem as how confident people feel about their relationships, women would outscore men.

~56% of women compared to 41% of men feel that they are a good friend.

~54% of women compared to 46% of men feel that they are a good worker.

~48% of women compared to 38% of men feel that they are a good parent and ~36% of women compared to 22% of men that they are able to express emotions

In order of importance, there are the four keys to sexual self-esteem:
1. Satisfied with body and looks
2. Have paid work
3. See work as successful
4. Rate self as attractive

American women value independence, self-sufficiency and being unique. In relationships, women have considerable strengths that often go unnoticed or unrewarded by the male dominated society.

Being interdependent, seeing themselves in a relation to other people makes women feel good about themselves. If a women had designed the presently used self-esteem, test men would be trying to explain their low opinion of themselves and how they should improve their self-image.

Even though women have a capacity to feel pity for others by seventy-two percent, it is difficult for them to feel sorry for themselves. As a group, women generally expect great things of themselves and are not tolerant of their own shortcomings. Feeling sorry for ones self is usually seen as negative, but it is in fact a key ingredient to a healthy self-esteem.

TWO KINDS OF WOMEN

The differences between women with high self-esteem and those that scored low on the traditional scale of self-esteem are that high self-esteem women are likely to:

~feel in control of life almost all the time

~have power at home

~have power at work

~use talents to fullest

~feel creative

~feel satisfied with:

        motherhood

> friendships
> marriage or love life
> spiritual life
> be a college graduate
> earn $30,000 or more

Low self-esteem women are likely to:

~be overweight

~call self names

~agree that "no one knows the real me"

~Liked self if:

> got more exercise
> lost ten pounds or more
> were smarter
> earned more money
> got more respect from children
> spouse appreciated them more
> got listened to more

Women named things during my interviews that are most important on their list of why they like themselves. They indicated that they are:

*a good parent

*a good friend

*are understanding

*have a lot of love to give

*are faithful

*are dependable

*have the ability to forgive someone

*believe in God

Women agree that family relationships are most important, but that their work and friends are a close second.

SEXUAL APPETITE

Of course you relish sex. Most people who have become involved in sex have a sexual appetite. Many topics of conversation between women and men have sexual overtures. As difficult as it is to believe, having sex is fun and can be pleasurable all the time. Any woman can experience a full and rewarding sexual appetite, especially if you have discovered your sexuality in a positive way. Statistically speaking, most women are said to reach their sexual prime a point in their lives between twenty eight and thirty five years of age. They either love to have sex or the idea of having sex.

A woman who has learned to be in tune with her sexual appetite and has the ability to understand her sexual moods is a woman who appreciates her body and the pleasures that can be attained from its appreciation.

Before women can began to understood the value of their sexual appetite they must get in tune with their sexual moods. Women should chart their wants, needs and desires on a monthly calendar. I charted and found that three to four days before my period, I was dormant sexually and had no desire to be kissed or touched by my lover. This usually lasted two days, but as soon as my period began I was as horny as a toad. When you have to have sex and you get it when you want it, do you masturbate? Are you sexually high in the mornings, low in the evenings? Do you find yourself waking up in the mornings yearning for his caress, his penis or his touch? Are you most erotic around the fifth of the month? Do you find that fatigue or worry make you want to cuddle with him? When alert and happy, do you want to make love all day long? When you drink alcohol, do you want romance more than sex? Do you prefer wild, passionate sex whether romance is present or not? Do you know which kisses turn you on and which turn you off? If you've never charted these things or haven't paid attention to your sexual senses, begin today by keeping personal records of your body's moods and sexsitivities. You'll be surprised at what you learn about yourself. Chart for approximately three to four months and the things that you've never paid attention to will begin to alert your sexual awareness.

After a few times with your lover, chart your sexual desires, your dislikes and likes. Record your ups and downs, your highs and lows. Rate your sexual partner from one to five. This is your own personal rating. He never has to know that he's being rated. No one can tell you what is good and what is bad. It's all up to your sexual appetite and what it takes to please you and YOU ONLY. Everyone is responsively different, so don't expect your sensitivity to rate the same as your best friend's, your sister or anyone else. Jot down the times of day that your body is most responsive or most sexually excited. If you are dedicated to listening to your body's responses, you will awaken your body's sexual aptitude and you will learn how to read your body's sexual signs and signals. This will enable you to appreciate yourself and to use your sexual appetite as long as you are sexually active. Besides, think of all the sexual pleasures that are awaiting you. Ummmmmm, the thought of it all feels good.

SEXUAL MYTHS

In a basically good relationship, having little or no sex may be an important factor or problem. Sometimes you'll have it all and most of the time you won't. Too bad, but it won't be the end of the world. Relationships come and go. Good ones as well as bad ones.

Sexual taboos, myths, and lies that may be getting in the way of stimulating a better relationship with your partner can be dispelled. Some sexual myths are as follows:

Myth #1: Automatic arousal is necessary before sex is enjoyed.
Fact: Sexual arousal is stimulated by fondling, touching, rubbing, kissing, and a possible erotic mental imagery. Failing to focus on your sensory input can interfere with arousal due to negative thinking or distractions.
Myth #2: Sex should not be scheduled.
Fact: If sex is spontaneous fine, but if during the course of a busy day it can't be spontaneous, scheduling is the next best thing. At least you can plan the romance and the atmosphere where it takes place. Anything you think is worth doing can be scheduled and preplanned.
Myth #3: You can't get turned on by a best friend or a sibling.
Fact: Bull! If you lack imagination this might be true, but it's a natural part of evolution to be thrilled by someone you already know quite well. You can get turned on by thoughts of someone other than your lover as you make love to your lover.   All that's needed is a little imagination and initiative.
Myth #4: Intercourse is the ultimate to sexual satisfaction. Anything else does not count as good sex.
Fact: Sexual relations involve physical contact, whether it be touching fingers, toes, ears, eyes or mouth. Erogenous zones are all over the body and to enjoy sex does not mean that you must be penetrated. You can experience physical connections and sensuality when we snuggle, hug or hold hands. The erotic sex, intercourse and orgasms are options that could create pleasurable consequences. Emphasis on these things will create sexual dysfunctions with a man trying to desperately to slow down his orgasm with a woman that hurries to get hers.

Myth #5: If one person is turned on, love-making can be just as satisfying.

Fact: Pleasure is possible if only one person is turned on if the partner isn't resentful. It's acceptable for one person to be aroused by stimulation from the other without both partners being aroused. Even if both partners are sharing in the love, every love-making session can be successful. Not every session will be fulfilling for both partners everytime no matter how many times you make love.

Myth #6: It's unwise and artificial to try out new things.

Fact: Trying new and refreshing things is one of the best ways to keep love, romance and sensuality alive and steamy in a relationship. Each partner should participate in the process of implementing new and wonderful things in their romance. If only a few of your sensuous physical experiments produce erotic sensations ---FANTASTIC! By increasing the ways that you expand your sex life can keep it exciting and refreshing.

Myth #7: If a woman takes the lead in sex it can damage her partner's ego.

Fact: Men and women are more flexible and free in their love-making these days. If men tell themselves that a woman is too aggressive for taking the lead, then they might well believe that this is so. Anxiety might result, which, in turn, can cause a decreased sexual enjoyment.

Myth #8: Overweight partners are unattractive and you can't get turned on by them.

Fact: Having someone who has a gorgeous body doesn't always bring sexual satisfaction. An overweight person can be sensuous, romantic and great in bed, whereas a beautiful bodied person can be lousy because he's stuck on himself. Some people with the most beautiful bodies are sexually gratifying. Many times an overweight person will work extra to please his partner because of his lack of so-called body qualities.

Myth #9: Having sexual fantasies about anyone other than your mate is abnormal and disgusting.

Fact: Sexual fantasies can be triggered by a variety of sexual responses and stimuli, including the way your partner touches, smells, thinks, or just about anything else. There isn't one particular thing or reason that brings sexual fantasies to the surface. The significance of it all can be quite rewarding. Women have sexual fantasies to increase or enhance their sexual experiences. Although some fantasies may be considered weird or bizarre they should not be seen as abnormal or disgusting. Some people even see them as cheating, but who's to say what is really cheating!

Myth #10: Having to tell your partner what you want isn't necessary. You shouldn't have to touch yourself at all.

Fact: Many women feel that if they have to touch themselves or tell their partner's what they want it means that they are non-sensuous or inadequate as a lover. This is not true because each partner's brain is tied into his or her own physical sensations. The secret of good sex is to share specifics of likes and dislikes without judgment or criticisms during love-making. Keep experimenting to learn exactly what your lover wants most. Once you've learned the things that turn your partner on, it can be a tremendous value to enhancing your arousal and orgasmic threshold.

Myth #11: Sex should be man on the top , woman on the bottom to get full satisfaction.

Fact: Sex can be enjoyed in many different positions.

Myth #12: You have to be available to make love with him at his requests.

Fact: Forcing yourself to make love when you aren't in the mood is wrong. It only brings bad memories into your love making arena. Keeping him interested even when you don't feel like it is the best remedy. Don't neglect him or tell him that you don't feel like it, but always make him feel desirable.

Myth #13: All men want sex.

Fact: Men want more than sex. They want physical, emotional and mental stimulation from their lover. Kissing, hugging and touching is quite sufficient for many men.

Myth #14: You can't teach an old lover new skills in the bed.

Fact: Most women confess that their lovers are willing to try new and exciting things in bed simply because they want to experience new things also.

Myth #15: Bad sex is better than none at all.

Fact: Having bad sex is not better than no sex because bad sex can compound any negative feelings.

Myth #16: Men like sexually aggressive women.

Fact: Men like sensuous women who flirt, tantalize and tease. Once initial contact is made he prefers her to step back and let him take over. They don't want women who take over the relationship.

Myth #17: Older couples have the best sex.
Fact: You can't make love forever so you might as well do it for as long as
you can. Older women do have an advantage because they are usually
in tune with their sexuality. Getting in tune takes a little longer for
some women.
There are many, many more myths that are circulating in the sexual arena,
maybe you've even heard a few that caught your attention. The most important
thing to remember about myths are: acknowledge them and communicate with
your lover as you experiment. Revitalize your love-making as you revitalize
your life and have fun in love as well as in love-making.

SEXUAL ETHICS

Every sexually active woman must take responsibility of her sexual actions.
There will be many times that she will want to spread her legs and get involved
with a man who's not right for her ethically.
Good judgment is necessary to keep dignity as well as integrity intact. Since
ethics are a very personal thing, a woman should consider them one of her most
important personal assets. The code of sexual ethics relates to your entire
approach to sexual encounters. Every woman has secret codes that she caters to
as she sets her standards. Having a conscience should also serve as a part of
your code of sexual ethics. Here are a few to get you started in the right
direction. Add to this list as you develop your own code of ethics.

1. **DON'T BE A GOSSIP.**
   Sexual gossip can hurt the woman more. Sex should be beautiful,
   therefore your sexual habits are to be cherished and remembered as
   such.   Don't allow your ego to spoil your pleasures by gossiping.
2. **KEEP YOUR HANDS OFF OF YOUR BEST FRIEND'S MAN.**
   Don't flirt or send out sexual signals to a man that you know belongs
   to one of your friends.   If, on the other hand, you want to end the
   the friendship go for it. However, this is not a favorable practice of real
   women. People have feelings.

3. **DON'T GIVE IN SENSUOUSLY TO MEN YOU DON'T WANT.**
Don't get in the habit of letting men touch you who have no feelings for you, even if he's your husband.

4. **GIVE TO HIM COMPLETELY IF YOU LOVE HIM.**
If you honestly love him give yourself to him completely. If he's the type that disrespects you or belittles you and is bad for you

5. **DON'T FALL IN LOVE WITH MARRIED MEN.**
This one is easier said than done. He's probably the dream boat who you've been looking for all your life, but he's married and you can't have him or can you? There are plenty of single, fine men who want loving and are willing to give good loving in return. Married men can't sleep over, it's difficult for them to go away weekends and they have limited activities to share with you. Even married women can't completely enjoy an affair with a married man, but it does have it's benefits. The expectations are equal and not as one sided as in an affair with one partner being married and one who isn't.

6. **DON'T TEASE OR LEAD ON IF YOU DON'T WANT HIM.**
If there is no physical or emotional attraction to him, don't play games with his emotions. Why mistreat, torture or tease a man that you don't want or have no intentions of loving.

7. **DON'T TELL A MAN YOU LOVE HIM IF YOU DON'T.**
Don't lie to him in order to get screwed or to test his masculinity, or to get his money. I know that when a woman sets out to get a man she will do whatever is morally ethical to get him, but don't tell him you love him, especially if he's emotionally weak for you. If you can't have your way with him, don't sink so low that you say " I love you" just to get your way. Being a Real Woman does not give you the right or privilege to hurt people's feelings. You don't get a permit to do as you please. You MUST arrive at a logical set of ethics that are personal, positive and practical enough to follow. Keep them clear in your mind and whatever you decide is right or wrong will help to guide you in the right direction. You'll be better off in your sexual relationships. You'll save yourself grief and guilt trips down the road.

8. **DON'T EXPECT HIM TO PROVIDE THE ONLY MEANS OF BIRTH CONTROL**

A smart woman will also provide the necessary protection to avoid an unwanted pregnancy as well as sexually transmitted diseases.

9. **TAKE RESPONSIBILITY FOR WHAT YOU WANT**

Societies ideas about what's nice and what isn't nice has caused many women to miss out on what they really desire. The only way that some women escape this trap is when things develop in a way that they just happen. Unfortunately, reasons to accept compromised feelings without looking anxious and without taking responsibility for what might happen occur more often in the world of fictional romance than in our own. We have to face the fact that sometimes we want to do things that are according to our own society's standards as inappropriate. When we try to figure out who actually benefits from our conventional behaviors, most of the time no one does. Don't allow a lack of courage to prevent you from doing what you really want to do.

10. **DON'T PROJECT NEGATIVE SIGNALS**

A realistic woman knows that meeting the man she wants cannot be left to chance. She has to do her part in communicating that she is available. She should not be so distant that a man chooses to bypass her due to her negative persona. If a woman gives off the right signals and keeps an open mind toward men, she can project the correct signals to land a positive man of her choice.

11. **DON'T DISCOURAGE MEN FROM APPROACHING YOU.**

When you see a man you like, and he really turns you on, it's up to you as a woman to to go a step further and encourage him in a positive way to come closer. A man can still chase a woman until she catches him, but if she doesn't encourage him along the way he'll feel rejection and give up on the chase. Showing him that you are ready and willing is where a relationship often starts. A willing woman is difficult for a man to resist.

12. **DON'T DEPRIVE HIM OF THE CHANCE TO SPOIL AND WANT YOU.**

Once you know that he wants you, relax and enjoy the results of your work and the continued efforts of his work. Give the opportunity to spoil you. Most men enjoying the idea and the efforts involved in pampering a woman. For a man it's important to impress a woman, anytime and anywhere.   A woman should never offer to pay for half of the meal that she just enjoyed.   Even if you earn just as much or more is no reason you can't adore his generosity. Enjoy all of his admiration and give him the proper time to desire you by giving him the proper attention.   Let him be uncertain whether you will make love to him when you two finally get together.

13. **<u>BE SURE THAT WHAT YOU GET IS WHAT YOU WANT.</u>** Insecurities, disappointments and doubts often make women settle for less than they deserve.   When you find a man that you are attracted to, don't let your feelings run away with you.   Try to be cool and don't get over anxious about him.   Don't ever feel that you are lucky to have him. Remember that he should feel lucky to have you. Look at where you are, and why you are there, and then be grateful that you have a right to make your own decisions and choices in a relationship.   Pay attention to the initial stages of a relationship so that failure can be avoided. Let your mind speak as clearly as your feelings. This will assist in preventing future pain and suffering later on down the road.

Chapter 22

VAGINA:

TM

YOUR SEXIEST ASSET

One of the most popular names in the world is VAGINA. This tiny yet powerful lovemaker has a scent that can weaken the strongest men. Just the thought of it can stiffen men to long hot grunts. The pride of most men is this wonderful and fantastic orifice.

Between a woman's legs is the most fascinating of all human organs. The vagina is the true tunnel of love. Many girls don't appreciate its size, but a woman will treasure its mere presence. This tiny hole that enlarges as a man's erection enters it is a pleasure center to be adored by all that possesses one. The muscles that make up the vaginal walls have the capacity to hold onto your lovers penis as it enters you. It is called the barrel of the vagina. This area is like a barrel heaped with muscles that are crucial to pleasing a man.

Youth brings tight, taut and gripping residence. Growing older and bearing children causes these muscles to become loose and slack. Men prefer tighter vagina's. Rest assured there are ways to keep it tight and trim to please the both of you.

EXERCISING THE VAGINA

One of the best ways to keep the vagina tight and trim are to exercise wherever you are. No matter what you're doing you can contract your muscles for at least an hour or so each day. Controlling vaginal muscles will become easier if you exercise them regularly. Developing the snatching motion with these muscles will add appreciation and excitement from your lover. Keeping the muscles in shape takes time, practice and consistency.

Practice can be great if you find a plastic penis-shaped vibrator or another hard object that is approximately the same size as a man's penis. Insert the new found object into your vagina and, using only your muscles, began to squeeze inward. Be sure to clean the object thoroughly before usage. Continue to do this exercise daily until you can shoot the object out of you like a firing bullet. Set a goal to shoot it ten feet. Once your vaginal muscles have been trained, they are very powerful.

Some women have trained their muscles to the firmness of reciting musical tunes. Some have even toned their vaginal muscles to the tightness of squirting fluids up to thirty feet, or picking up coins from the floor. You may not want to develop your vaginal muscles to this point, but it sure can work wonders in bed. Having a tight and trim vagina to accompany your love-making is great for your lover also.

When a man's penis comes in contact with your vagina you can use your vagina to caress him, stimulate him, excite him, control him and eventually bring him to a climax. Getting your vaginal muscles into shape should be one of your most important missions as a sensuously attractive woman. The next thing to do is operate them as sensuously successful as you possibly can.

A man will feel many sensations in his penis as he enters your vagina. When the head of his penis (the glans) bumps its way past your inner lips, or your labia minora, it becomes easily swollen with blood, causing sexual excitement. As the male plunges his penis into your vagina he will feel a soft, wet, warm, and clinging sensation on the entire length of his penis. Practicing your vaginal exercises on his penis will bring wonderful sensations.

VAGINAL MUSCLES

When your vaginal muscles are flexed he will feel a sensation on his penis somewhat like a small hill with a speed bump. As he receives full stimulation from making love, a combination of sensations are felt by you.

> swollen labia minora
> moist vaginal interior
> extra tantalization from your taut vaginal muscles
> suction from your hungry vaginal muscles

Your muscles will contract when you reach a climax. These muscles that you feel he also feels which should be pleasurable for the both of you. When a woman climaxes she doesn't squirt her fluids as a man does, she secretes liquid from her vaginal walls quite freely.

Since the vagina has a distinct smell to it, you have nothing to worry about. A woman should worry if she doesn't have a smell because the purpose of fresh vaginal odor is to arouse a man. Many woman find this fact hard to believe, but what really turns a man on is the smell of a well-lubricated vagina. Women who use deodorants would be doing themselves a sexual disfavor as well as harm due to the sensitivity of the vaginal tissues. Your freshness should be attractive, not offensive or old. The myth that vaginas smell like fish, started because of an unclean vagina.

Secretions from the vagina are clear or slightly milky. Anything else deserves a check from your doctor. Lubrication for comfortable love-making can be used to stimulate the flow of vaginal secretions.

VAGINAL SENSATIONS

Sometimes words are not enough when discussing sexual organs. All women should have enough nerve to pose naked in front of their mirrors. They should examine themselves in great length. Many woman give men that privilege before they've taken the privilege themselves.

Sit down or lie down with your legs spread apart. Separate your vulva (outer lips) as far as you possibly can. The parts of the vagina that are visible is the vulva. At the lower section of your vaginal lips is the entrance of the vagina which is, usually where the penis penetrates during sex. The internal lips are called the labia minora which get full of blood and swell to a beautiful puffy fullness when sexually aroused. Above the vagina is the urethral opening, which is a very tiny opening. Above the urethral opening is a pyramid shaped hood that the meeting of the lips form. Within these lips is a pea shaped bump called the clitoris. Whether your clitoris is large or small you do have one. Many people have difficulty finding it because of its hidden quality, especially men.

Just as a man has a penis, a woman has a clitoris. When it is aroused it gets swollen, just as a man's penis does. It gets swollen stiff and very sensitive. The clitoris is a small part of a large organ, which is hidden inside the female. Stimulating the clitoris physically turns women on and, whether direct or indirect, stimulation causes excitement in this tiny sex organ. The excitement that comes with penile penetration as your lover slides in and out of your vagina has many benefits to the clitoris by rubbing up against it or brushing his hairs against it. This leads to pleasant sensations as it pulls on the labia minora and again against the clitoris.

The simple pressure of a man's pubic bone is enough stimulation to excite the woman to a climax. Most women can use direct stimulation to bring themselves to an orgasm. This is called masturbation. The problem is not with women bringing orgasms to themselves, it is with whether or not men can stimulate the clitoris properly enough to bring a woman to orgasms.

Before any woman can expect a man to bring her to those fantastic and glorious sensations she should be able to bring herself to orgasmic heights. Besides, how can a woman tell a man where to touch if she doesn't know.

You can help your partner by guiding him through the art of satisfying you by using masturbation techniques. It takes years for some women to find their clitoris. When they finally discover this pleasure button... they are ecstatic. Some ways that are useful for lovers to share in stimulation are:

1. Sexual devices called clitoral simulators that help arouse.
2. Tongue kissing the clitoris.
3. Vibrators.
4. Massagers.
5. Rubbing or self-stimulation.
6. Having your mate to rub your clitoris.
7. Water from a faucet running onto your clitoris.

Don't stimulate your clitoris everyday manually or during love-making or it will become difficult to climax with direct stimulation. Getting this extra boost is nice, but don't allow clitoral stimulation to be your only source of satisfaction to achieve essential satisfaction in sex. It will eventually become a nuisance. Whether your clitoris is large or small has no bearing on your erotic stimulation.

VAGINAL TRICKS AND PALPITATIONS

Oh.....the things that you can do with those vaginal muscles. Some women think that in order to climax you have to be manually stimulated by your lover.   This is far from the truth. If you are having sexual intercourse and all you're receiving is a sore vagina, I don't need to tell you that something's wrong.   Things don't have to be this way.

Every woman has a sex sense, but it, just as the other senses, must be trained through some physical experiences to fine tune it. With practice you learned to dance on beat. With practice, you will also learn to control the rhythm of your vaginal muscles. Using the proper vaginal palpitations will add tantalizing sensations to your lover's penis. To help you build up your confidence in your sexual ability, your sexual senses must be greatly enhanced.

The vaginal tricks used to practice on your palpitations were all designed by women who have tried and tested their methods. These palpitations will help to bring addition pleasures while making love.

Number One:

While douching, place your vaginal syringe at the tip of your vagina and with the suction of your vagina squeeze and pull the syringe in with your muscles only. If you are doing this properly your vagina will act as a vice and grip the syringe as it cleanses your vagina. It will suction water from the syringe and cleanse you simultaneously. You can practice this method each time you douche, so you'll get vagina exercises to improve palpitations even while cleansing.

Number Two:

While masturbating, suction your vaginal muscles in and out as tightly as you can. This method adds sensitivity and stimulation to your clitoris as you masturbate. The suctions and palpitations strengthen your vaginal walls, therefore increasing the gripping tendencies of your entire vaginal muscles.

Think of silk when you touch your mate.

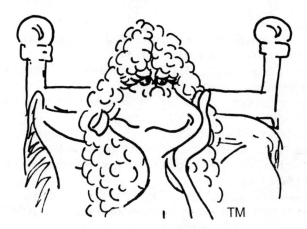

Chapter 23

DISCOVERING YOUR CLITORIS:

PLEASURES

If you really enjoy having your clitoris stimulated then this chapter is for you. Even though many women enjoy clitoral stimulation, most from this group prefer indirect clitoral stimulation in gentle circular motions from the hand or tongue. Imagine these movements surrounding the clitoris as he rhythmically plays with it. Stimulating the clitoris helps women to achieve orgasms. Even though men are still confused about the actual location of the clitoris and how it should be touched, they manage to find its vicinity. With all the publicity surrounding the clitoris, it's a wonder men as well as women, worship it. Even the unsureness of its complete function brings excitement. Stimulation to the clitoris directly or indirectly has helped many women achieve orgasms during sexual intercourse. Men feel that they can make a woman come without direct clitoris stimulation, whereas most women surveyed felt that the stimulation was needed to achieve an orgasm.

Indications are that the clitoris is still a mystery in spite of all the articles and research done to explain its significance, location and stimulant requirements. Men don't seem to understand how to proceed since women fake orgasms. Men are mystified by the clitoris and men fear that they are too rough or not rough enough, and they sometimes feel that they are not manly enough to bring their women to orgasms with their penis.

Don't continue to deny your needs to yourself or your lover's. If you want your clitoris stimulated you must let your lover know. If you are close enough to be having sex, then you're close enough to ask for what you want from your lover.

Few men will admit that they experience difficulty finding a woman's love button. To find the clitoris, use this simple method: **SHOW HIM.** Since many men feel uncomfortable asking for directions to the clitoris the woman should show him freely as a natural part of love-making. A woman has a personal right to show her lover what she wants. Have the man to pull away the fleshy part of the labia with one hand and as he wets his finger he should began circular motions alternating with a back and forth motion. If he uses this motion he won't miss any parts of your clitoris. You may be a little shy at first, but after the initial showing and guiding of his hand, you'll feel more comfortable. Even though everyone is different, men naturally seek out the easiest approach. This approach usually works on most women.

Once a women has become acquainted with clitoral stimulation she craves it. One of the most popular clitoral stimulations is the use of your lover's tongue in long slow strokes horizontally along the clitoris sides. The hand is usually the least popular stimulant because the hand tends to be rough and without constant lubrication, it can scratch or scuff the clitoris. The tongue is nicer because it is naturally lubricated and it's also softer. The tongue can get into tiny crevices of the clitoral area that are difficult for the finger to manipulate. Lubrication is very important to the clitoris. Even if the hand is lubricated, it doesn't seem to manipulate or stimulate the clitoris as well as the mouth or tongue.

The use of the tongue is almost always sure to turn you on. The hand and finger pressure is often a negative factor with the main complaint being they are either too rough or not hard enough. Some men have learned to combine their hand, finger, and mouth stimulations. This method is one of the most effective stimulants of the clitoris. Using the middle finger to make soft figure eight motions by the man can drive a woman to ecstasy. He can kiss her back while stimulating her clitoris. He can kiss her stomach, navel and breast as he stimulates her clitoris.

Other methods can also be experienced. He can nibble, lick or bite her buttocks while stimulating your clitoris also.

The best methods of all methods are those that you and your lover invent. Don't allow him to cause you pain or discomfort while trying to please you. The clitoris is very sensitive and some women do not like or need direct stimulation.

Most women I interviewed liked direct clitoral stimulation. Women who enjoy clitoral stimulation can enjoy it even more if they would help to guide their lovers in the right direction. Now that you know the penis is not the ultimate satisfier and the clitoris is the key to the female's orgasm, we can give the clitoris its fully deserved credit. Don't become a my-time-your-time love-maker to your lover. Become a total part of your sexual delight, whether through manual or oral stimulation. Help your lover to get you to the edge of climax then stop and allow him to use his hand, finger or mouth before he makes love with you. You'll be so hot that the grinding and rubbing will bring each of you off. The main thing is to get yours first and then help him to get his as you get yours again. Believe in yourself, believe in your orgasms and believe that your pleasures are natural, needed and beneficial.

Good performance is lasting.

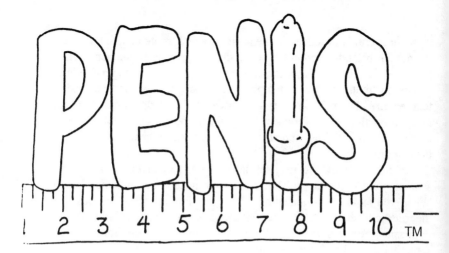

Chapter 24

PENIS

The penis is the basic area on a man that can be counted on to bring fantastic sensations. Most women know that this area is full of sensitive nerves bringing intense sensations.

Between those masculine legs of your man is this fabulous, extraordinary and powerful piece of one hundred percent beef. Many myths surround this infamous piece of meat. The mere presence of a man will cause women to discretely discuss the bulge in his pants. Though it has many names, (the penis, dick, cock, dingus, wang, pecker, toolie, john, willie and thing) they all stand for the same erotic object of a woman's desire.

Actually to a real women the actions and proportions of the penis are not difficult to understand. The penis is not difficult to interpret either. The penis for simplicity is nothing more than a rounded, lengthy sponge that fills when sexually aroused. Inside the shaft of the penis is a network of spongy tissues that fills up with blood. There is a valve that restricts the blood from leaving the penis too soon. This causes the shaft to be hard and swollen, which, in turn, creates an erection. The rounded head of the penis, also known as the fireman's helmet because of its shape, is full of sensitive nerves that respond naturally to friction and rubbing. The most sensitive part of this organ is the frenum, a thin piece of skin located behind the opening in the end of the penis.

Male sperm is produced in the testicles which some people know as the nuts or balls, located in the pouch that hangs beneath the penis. The purpose of them dangling freely in the breeze is because the production of sperm requires lower temperatures than that of normal body temperature. The balls are wrinkled because they help to radiate heat away from the balls, helping to keep them cool. When cooled, your man's balls may tighten and shrink. This is because heat is kept in by the scrotum.

Sperm made by the testicles later proceed up a tube where the seminal fluid is produced. The sperm is protected and nourished here. When you lover is stimulated this fluid goes into the tube that runs up the middle of the penis and the sensations start off a muscular reaction of spasms. The semen is then comes out in about four squirts that can sometimes travel as far as ten feet or more.

The bladder is closed off during erection of the penis simultaneous ejaculation and urination is impossible. Erections don't actually hurt, but they do feel tingly and swollen to men. Some men have morning erections known as morning glory. This erection is caused by a full bladder and should not be considered an erotic interlude.

As many things that can cause an erection can cause a downfall of one. Alcohol can make a man feel enlarged, but can cause "brewers droop." Narcotics and tranquilizers do the same.
Anxiety and tension due to worries can also cause a limp penis, so to speak. .

If your man experiences penis downfall, reassure him that all is okay by continuing to give love and affection. Don't complain or criticize him about his inability to get an erection. Joking isn't nice nor is it appropriate. Be tolerant of him and soon his penis will get an erection.

If his penis still doesn't grow, encourage him in a positive and hopeful way to see a doctor. Trying to increase his penile erection with gadgets may cause him to grow dependent on them without resolving his problem.

PENIS SIZE

The average size of the penis is about six inches long when erect. The longest penis in the world is recorded as fourteen inches. It was last seen in East African Bush. Your vagina will be able to accommodate an average penis plus a few inches more. After all, babies come from this opening. You'll have no trouble fitting your lover even if he looks larger when on hard.

endings. The most sensitive part of all the penis parts is the frenum, the string like vein located on the underside of the penis.

Some men have anxiety problems because they feel that their penises are too small. Women and men take the value and size of penises very serious. What they fail to realize is no matter how small, large, or well hung a penis size, the size is not really a factor in sexual intercourse. The size of a man's penis is not a problem for the woman who knows that she can be equally satisfied by any penis as long as the man who owns it knows how to use it. Since so many women tend to worry about the tightness of their vagina or the size of their breasts, the least of their worries is their man's penis size.

Penis size has become a tiresome obsession. The man who carries the lightest load between his legs is usually embarrassed by it and feels insecure on most occasions. If your man thinks his penis is too small, don't allow him to hassle with hormones, vacuum pumps or other contraptions because they have been proven not to work for enlargement, although they been noted as building a man's ego.

Don't let your man pad his crouch; false advertising will hardly make your man's insecurities leave. It will only cause disappointment later. The woman can play an important role in helping her lover to recognize the other good aspects of his penis size.

Since penises vary greatly in length, width, and shape, some are straight when erect, others curve back or sideways. Obsession with size by men only serves to reduce him to a statistic, and society is already too preoccupied with quantity of human beings. Whatever the size of the penis, it is worthy of its limited functions and it is fully capable of giving you pleasure if you are not too big in your vaginal area.

A French physician by the name of Dr. Jacobus made a survey of penis size in Africa. He was the French army surgeon who went from village to village measuring the size of any man's penis that gave him consent. My question is how did this doctor feel measuring all these dicks?

FACTS ABOUT PENIS SIZE:

Some important facts for women to remember when they get too preoccupied with penis size is:
1. A man's penis size in its dormant state is not much bigger in it's erection state, and a small penis in its dormant state is usually bigger in its erection state.

2. No matter what the size of his penis, that is not the only tool used to arousea woman. To be honest, penises aren't really good for anything, but poking sensuously in and out of you. They are inflexible when hard, and they have no protruding surfaces.

3. When making love with a woman, the real sexual organs on a man that are most effectively used on a woman are his hands, tongue and his. Whatever the size of your man's penis, it's deserving of its limited functions and it's fully capable of giving woman the pleasures that it was meant to give.

Once a woman realizes that her man is not sexually limited physically, he'll have to stop giving her lame excuses for not being able to be a complete sexual partner. He'll have to also rid himself of those self-defeating feelings of inadequacy that have deprived her of sexual fulfillment.

Practice will help you to find out how firmly he wants to be caressed or touched. You should also keep in mind that the head of his penis is the most sensitive area and it will respond to various degrees of pressure. The penis shaft has less sensitivity to it, so you can grip it, clasp it, or caress it with more strength. Men feel that women don't hold their penises with enough firmness when fondling or masturbating them. The tennis racket hold is said to be a good feeling. If you want your partner to really respond to your touching of his penis you should grasp with a tightening as you descend toward the base of his penis. (See penis Manipulations)

CIRCUMCISED vs. UNCIRCUMCISED

During the Roman Empire, a foreskin, uncircumcised or draped penis was important cosmetically to conform to the ideals of beauty. Athletic games required foreskin to cover the glans (head of the penis). Many athletes came from N. Africa and E. Mediterranean, where circumcision was common. Some physicians believed that circumcision discouraged masturbation, because it shortened the foreskin. Circumcision became popular in the United States in the 19th century for the same reason. Today circumcision serves no purpose and it certainly doesn't prevent masturbation though it is suggested and justified as a hygiene measure. A circumcised penis is thought to be easier to keep clean, but to clean an uncircumcised penis you would only need to spend a few seconds to get it perfectly tidy. When erect, circumcised and uncircumcised penises look and feel much the same.

Many women have refused or rejected uncircumcised partners or lovers because of the extra skin. The uncircumcised penis is not very attractive to many women that I interviewed and they felt that it was unclean as well as unhealthy to participate in sex with a man that was uncircumcised. This is a myth since most of them were born with an uncircumcised penis.

Sixty-two percent of the women I interviewed said that they wouldn't dare perform oral sex on an uncircumcised penis. This same group of women felt that an uncircumcised penis was unattractive and unsexy. This group also felt that it carried an odor that was not very enticing when making love.

Some men will experience the lack of a full erection due to the prepuce being too tight. This condition is called phimosis. Medical circumcision is required when the foreskin is too tight due to recurring infections.

Circumcision among adults can be very painful and serious and should not be taken purely for cosmetic reasons. Trying to circumcise one's self can result into mutilation and very serious infections.

If you happen to fall in love or even decide to make love to an uncircumcised penis here are a few things that you should remember:

1. Keep condoms available at all times.
2. Make sure your lover pulls the foreskin back and cleans it thoroughly with soap and water. You may choose to assist him in this effort on occasions so that he will be assured of your support.
3. Be sure to use a condom on his penis whether he is circumcised or uncircumcised. It's for the health of it.
4. If his penis possess odors that you are not familiar with, refuse to have sex until you investigate why.
5. Remember rule numbers one through three.

PENIS EXERCISES
Manipulations: Thrills, Chills and Spills

Some penile exercises that are sure to bring more control and stamina to your man's penis are:

1. Take a wet towel and wrap it around your man's penis. Have him to practice lifting the wet towel with his penis. **NO HANDS ALLOWED.** You can count as he lifts or he can lift in private. The object is to have him lift to a set number daily, after about a week or so you'll began to notice his penile thrusts being more

controlled and rhythmic as you make love. The control will heighten his pleasures. Have him practice on lifting other objects with his penis. After all it can only help.

2. Tell him that you have a special exercise just for him. Naked, have him stand the length of his penis away from you. If his penis is four inches while soft, have him to stand only four inches away. His objective is to try to touch you with his penis as he lifts it. He can't touch it with his hands and nor can you. He must lift to touch you twenty times in the beginning, and increase the lifts as often as needed. You may not make it to twenty before you want to have him make love with you, but try anyway. *Another variation of this one is to have him try to lift his penis to your mouth at least twenty times before you have sex. Kneel on your knees as he stands in front of you to play the game.

3. Spell your name on his penis as you administer oral sex. Here's how: Suppose his name is Joe Bob Baker, take your tongue and as you suck, lick, or fondle him with your mouth spell each letter on his penis with your tongue. You'll make each letter three to four times or maybe more because you'll spell it different ways. First spell it in cursive writing, then block style, then print it. You can stay on each letter for as long as you like. Naturally there will be times that the letters you are spelling out will feel better than others to you and him.A variation of this spelling game is:

Have him to spell his name on your clitoris with his penis head, or tongue.Make it more interesting by spelling the entire alphabet in cursive, block style or print. If you know how to write in calligraphy try it on his penis and then let him return the favor on your clitoris Incorporate your favorite writing skills to this game and the fun will be endless.

You can spell, draw or even sculpt on his head with your tongue, and besides think of all the good practice you'll be getting.

FLOPPY DICKS..not floppy disks

While women are concerned with their desirability as lovers, a man is asking himself several questions:
1. Will he be able to get an erection?
2. Will he be able to keep an erection?
3. Is he turning her on?

4. Did the last man she was with do it better?

In the past women have passively opened their legs to subject themselves to their partners sexual affections only to be disappointed to tears sometimes. Women are no longer willing to settle for JUST SEX. Women want sensuality, emotion and excitement from their partners. The women's capacity to have orgasms has caused an inferiority complex for men during sexual intercourse. Men fear the fact that women can have multiple orgasms compared to their one timers. The importance for men to be considered good lovers is obvious. A man's sexual self-esteem is related to orgasms and potency. Orgasm popularity has become somewhat of a burden to men and to find out that most of what he's been doing to please a woman sexually was wrong makes him a little insecure.

With all the hang ups men have before sex it's a wonder that they can get it up. By the time men get past their seductive stage and lure women to the bedroom they're devastation causes floppy dicks. Rather than express what's bothering them they'll say "this has never happened to me before." Some women felt that men avoided them after sexual problems occurred, and some women avoided men who didn't satisfy them on the first time.

If a man's penis says no, the sexual intercourse is practically out of the question, so women should learn to give other forms of physical attention in times like these.

WHAT TO DO WITH HIS PENIS (skills)

1. Roll his penis between the palms of your hands and knead it as if it were a piece of bread dough.
2. Press his penis against your pelvis.
3. Thump his penis against your belly, face or thighs.
4. Allow him to rub his penis between the cheeks of your buttocks.
5. Fondle his testicles as you rub your penis.
6. Press your finger or your tongue on the area between his anus and his scrotum. This spot is called the perineum. This spot stimulates his prostate.
7. Fondle him just because he's your man. While he's reading, talking on the phone, cooking, or doing handy work around the house is a good time to reach into his pants and fondle him.
8. Make two rings with your thumb and index finger of each

hand. Place them next to each other on the middle of his penis. Gently pull outward in both directions at once.

9. Without penetration, have him to rub his penis over the entire surface of your vagina very slowly.

10. Press your breasts together and let him slide his penis between them. Rub your breast across his body trying to stroke your nipples ever so lightly against his penis. He'll enjoy watching you manipulate his penis. A sensuous pleasure to top this would be to allow his penis to emerge from between your breast to your mouth.

Chapter 25

GREAT BALLS OF FIRE

What to do with those balls. In all cases where your lover's balls are concerned, the tongue forms one of the most important pleasure of all. Even though men like to have their balls gently stroked and caressed, a favorite is licking their balls. There are variations to the ways that you can stimulate the balls without causing pain to this sensitive area.

STIMULATION TECHNIQUES:

Some popular stimulation techniques applied to the balls are:

1. Stroking with the tongue from the underside to the topside.
2. Long to short licks and then long again.
3. Slightly place your massager or your vibrator on the underside of his balls, making sure you gently passing his anus as you began.
4. Gently cupping his balls into the palms of your hands as you caress and lick, lick and caress.
5. Rub or lick from his anus to his balls over and over again throughout foreplay and then again right before sexual intercourse.

6.   Gently blow on his balls as if to blow into a baby's eyes. The chill going onto his balls will send pleasurable chills up and down his spine.
7.   Humming his favorite tune on his balls will give him erotic shivers.   He won't be able to think of anything or anyone but you.
8.   Blowing on the balls as they are licked.

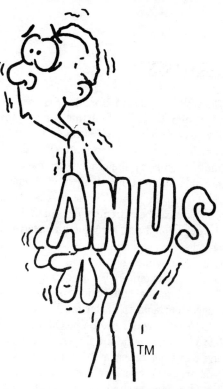

Chapter 26

ANUS
™

Culturally induced fears have given many people phobias about their assholes. This bias against the anus is unreasonable. True, it is used for elimination, but so is the vagina and the penis, yet the objection has not made the latter any less attractive. The anus is not only an avenue for elimination, but also a sexual organ. It's highly sensitive as it is lined with particularly responsive nerve endings. Moreover the male anus is close to the prostate gland which when stimulated is extremely pleasurable to men. Traces of bowel can be banished if one takes the precaution of an enema before intercourse.

Every drugstore sells disposable enemas, but don't get caught up in the daily use of enema's, because it could create physical damage to the small intestine.

Anal sex is becoming quite popular with sexually active couples. People who are just beginning to try anal sex usually have a fear that sticking a penis up the anus will tear the skin. With proper lubrication and relaxation, pain and damage will be prevented. Losing muscle tone due to repeated anal sex has not been proven.

Some women go through guilt trips because they enjoy anal sex. They feel that only gay men get probed in the anus. Since women have found pleasure in their assholes, feelings of guilt are historically wrong.

ANAL SEX

The well-known area around the anus is an important erogenous zone that is stimulating to both men and women. Sometimes a woman enjoys having a man put his finger in her anus during intercourse and especially just before her orgasm. The idea of being penetrated twice is a true turn on and quite erotic when the timing is right. Many men also enjoy this stimulation. Women with long fingernails must be very careful not to nick the delicate tissues of the anus. Even the smallest tear of skin can be extremely painful in this area.

To began anal sex, a couple may start with frequent penetrations of each other's anuses and decide on intercourse later in the love-making session. If a women has not had anal sex before, it will take a few tries before she can comfortably accommodate a male's penis.

Oral and manual stimulations of the anus before intercourse will help to relax your anal sphincter muscle. Most women use lubricants such as: K-Y Jelly, Vaseline, Baby Oil, or Cold Cream. The man should dilate your anus with one finger, then two, and so on. Patience on the man's part is necessary at this time. Arousal should be slow and gentle. If you are not properly prepared, anal intercourse can be very painful. When you are excited and ready the man can start to enter you gradually, slowly and thoughtfully with his penis. He should not thrust, force or move too quickly at this time. Both his penis and your anus should be well-lubricated. He should bear down slightly on your anus to relax it and facilitate initial penetration. Men who enjoy anal intercourse with their lovers usually like the tight squeeze of the anus around their penises. This tightness makes penetration more difficult, so the man must not thrust or go too quick, nor penetrate too deeply. You as a woman must help to guide him in the right direction.

There are, as with any sexual act a few myths associated with anal sex. Anal sex is practiced by some women to simply avoid unwanted pregnancies, or to maintain virginity. In some cultures anal sex is considered illegal and sodomy.

ANAL SEX EXERCISES

Some couples do the following exercises in their bath tub because the warm water helps the woman to relax and the bathroom holds a rule of having privacy. Some of the women I talked to practiced alone at first, and later invited their lovers. Here are two suggested exercises:

1. Wash the anus, including just inside the anus with soap and water. Lubricate your finger with K-Y Jelly and insert it into the anus. As you began to relax, apply more lubricant and push deeper. Deliberately tighten your sphincter muscles and then relax again. You'll be quite surprised at the strength your sphincter muscles have. Grip, relax, grip, relax, several times over. You'll notice the change in the texture of your rectum. Move your fingers in and out a couple of inches at a time. If you're fearful about anal penetration, you'll be amazed at how easy it is if your lover is patient.

2. This exercise can be practiced with your lover ask him to explore your asshole with his fingers. Then put your finger in his ass. Jack him off with one hand while you insert one or two fingers of your other hand into his anus. As you masturbate him, move your fingers rhythmically in and out. Never put anything else into your anus. No glass bottles, small exotic objects, or dangerous solutions. These type of objects can possibly get lost in your intestines and require major surgery.

PREPARATIONS FOR ANAL SEX:

1. Physically, all you need to do is clean yourself out with an enema.
2. Have condoms ready and always insist that your partner wear them.
3. Do not use mind altering drugs or alcohol at this time due to alterations of your sensitivity.
4. Use good judgments about safe sex.
5. Choose a lubricant that contains nonoxynol-9.
6. Lubricate your anus and your partner's penis liberally.

HAZARDS OF ANAL SEX:

1. Not cleaning the anus before anal sex is unsanitary and unhealthy.
2. Transmitting bowel particles into the vagina of women can cause serious infections.
3. Breaking skin with rough anal sex can cause bowel movement discomfort.

ANAL SEX POSITIONS:

There's a couple of anal sex positions that you can start with. The easiest suggested position to start with involves both you and your partner lying on your sides. Sometimes the novice will prefer to be in control. In this position you face your partner who is on his back and you sit on his penis. Being on top will relieve your man of the anxieties that he will encounter from thinking that he may be entering too quickly. If you are on top you can control the rate of penetration yourself just remember that the average woman can accommodate a large penis in the vagina as well as the anus without difficulty.

When his penis is about a third of the way in, you may feel pain. Pull away gently and rest before trying again. The interval will give the sphincter time to open up. On the second attempt, you should be able to accommodate his whole penis. In fact you may be surprised at how easily it goes in. Remember to relax your entire body and all will go well.

The doggy style position is also a sexy position from the man's point of view. The man on top will continuously have a full view of your cheeks as he penetrates and he can watch his penis slide in and out as he penetrates you. He can allow his stares to wander all over your body as he gets turned on more at the thought of looking at your body from a different view. There are a couple of things that he can do: he can lean forward to wrap his arms around your stomach or he can massage your breasts with your hands to turn you on even more. In anal sex, touching and caressing is very important because it helps to relax the woman and it put her at ease.

Kissing your shoulders, nibbling your ears, licking your back and lots of caressing from your partner will add to the sensuous nature of this position. One of the disadvantages in this position is, it's very difficult to kiss face to face.

TM

Chapter 27

SEX:

WHAT'S NORMAL

The question that tends to come up the most about sex is "AM I NORMAL?" Most women are concerned with the normality of their sexual fantasies, responses, preferences, turnoffs, secrets and problems. Other concerns are the normality of their body features, and the frequency in which they want to have sex. The fear of being abnormal sexually can prevent pleasure and intimacy. Fear has consequences and is the basis for many versions of "Am I normal?" Women said things like:

 *My climax takes too long and that frightens me.
 *Should a man be able to keep an erection for a long time?
 *Do other people make love as often as I do?
 *Does the enjoyment of oral sex make me weird?

"Normal" means many different things to different people. People worry about what is statistically common; what our culture says is the right or wrong way in sexual behaviors. Sexual norms have been altered or changed within our life time. The acceptance of homosexuality, the clitoris, and even what is considered a wife's duties have all changed. Socially speaking, normal is what is socially accepted as normal by responsible consenting adults. What is not consensual is wrong, just as tricking someone to make love to you. Being irresponsible is wrong also. To expose a partner to a sexually transmitted disease is irresponsible, therefore it's wrong.

Society teaches children that sex is bad. Learning that sex is bad means that as sexual beings we are bad. These messages are derived from families, churches, synagogues and schools. Our environment teaches a child that sensitivity is somewhat abnormal also. Withholding sexual information from our children until they are grown, handicaps our sons and daughters. We want them to be intelligent, normal role models, but when they are sexually confused about their erotic feelings, we blame the sexual entertainment.

SEXUAL CUSTOMS

The United States has many laws governing sexual behavior. They have more than all the European nations combined. The only legally sanctioned sexual acts in the U.S. is private heterosexual intercourse between married adults.

The Oceanic societies have no words for indecent, obscene, or impure in their vocabularies. The topic on sex is not considered shameful or embarrassing.

Boys in Mangaia (a Cook Island) are given sexual instructions and taught the sexual techniques of various coital positions, breast stimulations, cunnilingus and methods of delaying ejaculation so that their female partners may experience orgasms.

The inhabitants of Bali and India have no elaborate practices of seduction. If sex is desired, one needs to simply ask. The Aweikoma of Brazil feel that since eating and intercourse involve body orifices the same term is used for both activities. The National Center of Health reports that seventy percent of married women have had premarital sex and that ninety-five percent of American women have had sex by age twenty-five.

Americans are exposed to some form of sexual innuendo about twelve times per hour or every five minutes. Tinquian people of the Pacific Islands do not kiss , but place their lips close to their partners and rapidly inhale.

This information was obtained from The Complete Book of Sexual Trivia by Leslie Welch.

WHAT'S TOO MUCH SEX

You think about sex often. You've just got to have it everyday. Could you be addicted to sex ? Wanting to sleep with an attractive stranger or even doing so doesn't make you a nymphomaniac, nor does the fact that you slept with an old boyfriend. In some of the worst relationships sex is sometimes the last thing to leave. Don't blame yourself for enjoying sex. Blame your sexual addiction on the new concept and over-publicized trend of sexual dysfunctions. Nationwide treatment for sex addicts are frequent. Many self-help groups which operate on the twelve step program principles are now forming. Sex addiction is considered a new disease and its treatments tend to make perfectly healthy women feel guilty just for having normal sexual desires. DON'T!! Listed is the **TWELVE STEP PROGRAM.**

ADDICT CONFESSIONS

Addicts are usually very easy to get into bed. Some of the things that tend to turn a sexual addict on are:
*Tieing wrists and ankles together or to the bedposts. Being bound excites these women.
*Being spanked during sexual intercourse with whips, belts or other abusive type paraphernalia is exciting to these women also. They get more excited with each slap or hit.

1. Expert Advice:
A growing number of experts share feelings about sex addiction and its treatment. Many believe that sex addictions are not "true addictions" but "only learned patterns of behavior" now stigmatized by our society. Researcher's reasons for their feelings are:
~Sex addiction is the only addiction in which a person is cured, as long as he or she uses "the drug"-sex- in an appropriate way, such as within a committed relationship.
~Repeated testing has found no differences between the mental state of sex addicts and non addicts.
~Even though the press blows sex related issues out of proportion, it is not listed in the Diagnostic and Statistical Manual of Mental Disorders because experts have not yet reached a consensus on its definition.
~Assessments of "sex addicts" tend to be subjective; moral or religious

values of the recovery group or therapist shape their diagnosis. Unfortunately for many women reawakened values have left them feeling guilty about their urges. Some women feel that their libido is just strong.

2. Escalating Sex Drive:

Some women admit that they have never been in a relationship that can completely fulfill their sexual needs. Many would make love every day if they could find a man to oblige their needs for that day. If intercourse or masturbation was not done in a few days, they compelled to go out and look for sex. Many experts feel that unless a women has to run to the restroom to masturbate because of the strong sex drive, nothing is wrong. They attribute this to her being more exciting in bed. Just because you want sex more than five times a week does not make you an addict.

3. Promiscuous Behavior:

Women who have sex with several partners in the same day or week are playing an unsafe game. Promiscuous behavior is not an indication of addiction. Women who have multiple partners without protection are risking their health. On the other hand sleeping with several partners can be a sign of problems.

4. Kinky Sex:

Rough sex is sometimes considered kinky. Some women have said that they don't need the kinky rough sex, but with the right man its a complete turn on. This same group of women craved to be dominated. Therapists agree that sexual behavior between consenting adults who don't cause serious pain or injury falls within the acceptable sex range. Kinky sex should cause concern if pain, violence or embarrassment is evident.

5. Impersonal Sex:

If you sleep with someone who you'd never think about dating, much less marrying, you're considered unbalanced. Going to bed with several men who, for various reasons, aren't people you'd like to see socially falls into this category. Some women have relationships for purely physical reasons. It's considered recreational love-making.

6. Easy Women:

Some men think that a woman who comes easy is EASY. Some women are so in tune with their wants, needs and desires that it doesn't take much for them to obtain gratification. Men label these women as nymphomaniacs. So do other women. Easy women don't necessarily need clitoral stimulation; and sometimes being kissed or touched in erogenous zones is enough to send them into ecstasy. These responses don't mark them as sex addicts-only lucky.

7. True Addicts:

True addicts are rare individuals. These are people that can't stop thinking about sex even after just having made love. After rejection by someone who you just had sex with, or cruel treatment from this same person and you still want to have sex with him in the next ten minutes or so is rare behavior. Women who are repeatedly driven to have sex, no matter how great the risk or humiliation, represent a tiny minority of the population, according to addiction theory's chief architect, Patrick Carnes. Carnes says the addict:

~Feels powerless" over her erotic urges, despite the risks.

~Knows deep shame and hopelessness.

~Experiences four distinctive phases during the "addictive encounter," from a trance-like state, in which an addict is intoxicated by the idea of sex, to the final phase, despair."

There are few women who fit this profile. According to Carnes, those who do have likely suffered physical, psychological, or sexual abuse as children.

A woman who feels good about herself can easily shrug off the "sex addict" stigma-even if a jealous friend or inadequate lover calls her one. A less emotional woman who is insecure might accept the labeling. For this reason alone their addiction is harmful.

Such pressures can hurt women more than it does men. Many women still have trouble taking charge of their sexuality. Women think that being the so-called "good girl" will help to earn these women love and acceptance. The thing to remember is that no matter how often you make love, it's nobody's business but your own.

TIPS ON SEX

Simple, but sensitive tips to unleash and enrich passion for your lover is an excellent way to liven up romance. It's up to you whether you accept pay for passion, or whether you just like the idea of it all. Don't toy with men knowing that you aren't going to have sex with them. On the other hand, if you know that you are going to someday have the pleasures of sex with him, then a little teasing won't hurt. These tips on sex will help you instinctively get back in touch with what you already know:

1. Pay Attention:
Today's life styles have made everything so easy to obtain that we have taken for granted one of life's greatest pleasures SEX. Our senses have become so dull because of all the other stimuli available. Listen to this stimuli, act on it, and enjoy it.

2. Create Mental Foreplay:
Even though physical foreplay is important in good sexual experience, mental foreplay is just as important. Plan ahead to eliminate the not in the mood syndrome. Surprise your partner with sexual invitations to sex. Don't wait on your partner to prompt you to think about sex. Put it in your schedule, and don't expect him to shift mental gears whenever you get the urge. Tell him about it ahead of time. Get him excited about your next time together. He'll be so excited by the time the two of you get together he won't be able to control himself.

3. Appreciate Your Body:
Perfect figures have caused women to lack esteem when it comes to their bodies. If you feel sexy, you'll look sexy. So think sexy because a body that feels sensual is a beautiful body. You're as beautiful as you feel.

4. Don't Expect Perfection:
Make love as good as possible, but don't think that it will be perfect every time. Sometimes even your best efforts will be pleasurable, but with your man they may not always be. Give yourself an A for having good intentions. Be patient and persistent in trying to improve your sex life. It won't change overnight, but it sure will be fun practicing to become better at it.

5. Don't Let Performance Take Over You:
Having orgasms is an objective of sex, but it doesn't have to be the only reason or the most important one. Too much focus on performance will stop natural response. Don't think so much about sex while having sex, because it distracts from being in touch with what is really happening.

6. Incorporate Teamwork in Sex:
Both partners must cooperate to reach their full sexual potential. Working as a team will bring more sexual satisfaction than working as a single unit. In sex you must be able to lead sometimes and follow sometimes, but it should be done in a cooperative manner because good sex is a team sport.

7. Use Your Senses In Sex:

Follow your instincts and appreciate the delicate senses that help you in sex. Taste and smell are probably the most delicate subjects for lovers to talk about, and are the most important when dealing with sex, especially oral sex.

Odors that are generated during sexual arousal are different for different people. Your attitude about odors will help you enjoy sex. Notice your partner's response to your touch. Be aware of how and where you liked to be touched. Revel in the sounds that you make. Don't hold them in and don't be embarrassed by sighs of pleasure. Notice the changes in his breathing; this is a good indication of when he's going to have an orgasm. Tuning in to each other during sex will help sexual experiences to be better for the both of you.

8. Be Open Minded:

Whatever you're doing now in sex is probably great, but it's not the only way to have sex. A quickie can be just as much fun as a full scale love session. There's nothing wrong with a hurried love session in the car if you're with a person who you love and care for. It's beautiful when you and your lover want sex at the same time waiting until you're secluded behind closed doors is not always appropriate as far as timing is concerned. Having a desire for sex when your partner does is a positive in any relationship. While your satisfaction is important, you can find pleasure in contributing to your partners satisfaction.

9. Don't Ever Neglect Sex:

Spontaneous or planned sex is okay. Planning helps during busy or hectic schedules. Spontaneity is great driving home from work with your lover if you can't wait to get home, pull over to the nearest motel and make love.

10. Don't Worry Unnecessarily:

One of the dangers in relationships is unnecessary worrying that keeps you from giving or receiving love without fear. Many women have hidden fears that are physical, mental or emotional. These fears stand in their way of enjoying their relationships.

SEXUAL WORRIES:

Some of the most common sexual worries are:

1. He doesn't enjoy my love-making anymore.

2. Are my breasts / clitoris / and vagina the normal size?

3. Is the lubrication of my vagina too much or too little?

4. I like rough sex, am I normal?

5. I have better orgasms when I masturbate, does this mean I'm a nymphomaniac?

6. I'm too fat to be loved?

7. He'd love me more if I were taller, shorter, thinner.

8. I need sex more than my partner.

9. I like anal sex, am I normal?

10. I like clitoral stimulation more than intercourse, am I normal?

11. Am I experienced enough for him?

12. This is too good to be true. It won't last.

Chapter 28

SEXUAL INTERCOURSE

When the big moment finally comes, a girl has got to be ready if she's going to enjoy it. The entire basis of intercourse is to receive sexual fulfillment and to give sexual pleasure to her partner. Love-making varies from person to person quite considerable. If you're accustomed to a man who keeps you screaming for more, another man's strokes and variations of thrusts could be very fulfilling or very disappointing.

POSITIONS

The missionary position where the man lies on top of the woman is the most effective position for the best sex. When a man supports his weight on his elbows in this position he has much more freedom to work his hip and body movement, and you can wiggle, scream, pull, bite or wrap your legs around his body with delight.

Guide his penis as he climbs on top of you so that you can help him to insert it into your vagina. If he has foreskin, you can gently peel it back as you give him an added sensation before insertion. As he begins to enter you, make it easy for by meeting him with your legs apart and your hips sucking forward to greet him at the deepest point of every stroke. You will help him as you are stimulated because his pubic bone will rub against your clitoris and deeper penetration into your vagina will be sensuously felt.

Women can control the strength of their erotic feelings during intercourse on all occasions and they sometimes don't know this. If you want to feel him penetrate you even more deeply inside, all you have to do is open your legs wider and then raise them. As his penis slides with an angle it will reach farther, giving the both of you more satisfaction. If you thrust upward and wrap your legs around his back as he pushes in, you may feel his penis tip touch your womb. Ummmmmmmmm, this will bring pleasures that you can't resist talking about. If you must talk, only talk about what you did to him, not what he did to you. You don't want any desperate and lonely women trying to get your man. . Too many women are guilty of running their mouths too much.

Rotate your vagina in circular motions, squares and/or alphabets at random, but don't tell him what you're doing. He'll scream out in a few minutes or so because the sensations that your rotations bring will weaken him sexually. As his penis is thrusting inward give him one of your sensuous circles and watch him twitch as you increase his pleasure. Find a common rhythm between the two of you and let the love motions flow.

Sexual intercourse and the length of time that you have sex is up to you. Suppose you would like to go on longer and if your partner is about to come here's a secret to delay his ejaculation. First, part your legs so that the pressure is lessened on his penis from your vaginal walls, and relax your vaginal muscles completely. Slow your hip movements down to a minimum grind and he will automatically slow down with you.

Intercourse is not supposed to be a ride on a roller coaster, starting slowly and then turning into a furious, crazy speed until he comes. Women have been trained and groomed to think that the man is supposed to control the sex as well as the love-making sessions, but you can change all of this by controlling him as you make love with him. Don't be one of the wham-bam-thank-you-mam-crew. Start off as slowly as you would like, work up an excitement of eroticism, then relax a while, change positions, get a drink or talk a while and start again. You can do this four or five times in a love session, to add variety to your pleasure. When the time comes for you to climax, try to change up your osition so that comfort will be the end result instead of freaky inventions of sexual positions. A woman tends to suffer female problems at no fault of her partner just because she is caught in an uncomfortable position at the time of climax. To enjoy the climax experience to the fullest, you must be able to feel the pleasure, not the pain of a contorted position. Besides, who wants to remember climax as a painful venture. That won't leave much room for joy or pleasure if you are constantly worried about pain the next time he wants to make love.

Love positions have such high levels of interest because, recently, the only way publishers could show positions was in an educational way. Only four or five effective intercourse positions are really effective positions for intercourse. In these positions you won't have to worry about pain or breaking an arm or twisting your neck.

THE MOST EFFECTIVE POSITIONS:

~You Underneath The Man

This position of all the sexual positions has the most going for it. It is by far the most basic, the most comfortable and the most loved position of all the sexual positions. Everyone's doing it. It's the easiest position to get into. It's the easiest position to control. It's the best position, even if you have a headache that he refuses to accept. It allows both partners pelvic rotations. It is the most personal of all positions because you actually are face to face with your partner. It's a bit hard on a man's elbows, but he still gets just as much pleasure because he's feeling dominant. But we know that you are the one in control because you are controlling the rotations. One female advantage is it doesn't require as much penetration to feel good.

~Man Underneath You

For the woman this position is perfect. The depth that the penis will go into you is controlled. You can lean forward for less depth and penetration or you can lean backward for inserting the penis deeper. This position allows you to pace and control the depth or the movements. If you decide that you want to squat on him, his frenum will be greatly stimulated. This is highly exciting. Men love this position but it is sometimes tiring to a woman's knees.

~Man Behind You As You Lie On Your Back

This position is sometimes called the scissors because of its positioning. It allows you to kiss your partner more completely as he caresses your breasts and your clitoris. Lift your legs and allow him to slide his penis into your vagina from a side angle. This unusual entry angle gives greater stimulation of the more sensitive parts of his penis, making up for the effort he has made, by allowing the weight of your legs to remain on him. Your cheeks act as a buffer making it difficult for your partner to enter your vagina as deeply as he would like. The disadvantage for the male is that he has to push himself with more effort in this position for the two of you to get maximum stimulation.

Most intercourse positions while sitting, standing or lying down are only variations of the basic positions. Many new ways can be invented with you and your partner using imagination. Even so, all of these positions still don't mean as much as having good sex.

Other more exciting ways of making love can be invented if you both put forth effort. Be sure that you put effort into your surroundings so that the atmosphere will be just as romantic as you are. Try to make him as comfortable as possible so that you can concentrate on the sensations of your vaginal contractions and palpations.

Trying every positions that you have ever heard of is fun, but if your setting isn't up to par, romance won't be as symbolic as you would like.

During sexual intercourse, your man's penis will rub against the walls of your vagina. From this, sensations are increasingly pleasurable and ejaculation is the height of satisfaction. The pleasures of his penis massaging you as he stimulates the clitoris will ultimately bring you to a wonderful climax.

Just as a man experiences an erection researchers have found that women experience an erection of the nipples while having a climax. This may not be true for all woman, even if she has just experienced an earth shaking climax.   It primarily depends on the woman.

Stopping in the middle of your love-making is a way to take a rest or change the pace. Know whether your lover comes slowly or quickly, then adjust your vaginal gestures to fit the need. Remember that you are the controller of the lovemaking, you only want him to think that he is. If you are sneaking a lovemaking session and time is a factor, I say by all means hurry. But make sure that even with your hastiness, you allow some passion to seep through that is thoughtfully romantic. Otherwise take your time to make it a memorable moment.

QUICKIES

Quickies are not always beneficial. Many men have used quick sex as a means to score or lay as many as they can in a given amount of time. They have been as shallow as to say that they felt this was all the woman wanted or they thought that she didn't need or want sexual pleasure. Quickies are the way men explained their deficiencies of not lasting longer in sex. But once you have read your Will The Real Women Please Stand Up, you can handle these deficiencies. Most men admit that they want lovemaking to last longer than it normally does. Some men even joke about how long it does last. If lovers are lucky, however quickies can bring lightning like pleasures.

Opposites attract, therefore women and men are naturally responsive to each other. Now days likes are attracting also, especially if there is a lot of things in common. Natural responses have brought many fabulous friendships together. In a passionate embrace that usually occurs while fully clothed, a quickie could naturally occur. Raw sensuality can unfold just by watching your man untie his shoe at the end of a busy day or as he works in the garage on his old car. Some of the most common ways to enjoy quickies are:

~standing against a wall or tree.

~leaning over a handy chair or table while receiving his penis from behind.

~having him sit on a chair as you straddle his lap with his penis inside of you.

~you can face your partner or you can sit on his lap or you can sit on his lap with your back to his face.

There are also several fantastic places to enjoy quickies, they are:

on a kitchen table	in a swimming pool
in a rocking chair	on a bathroom floor
on a kitchen sink	by a campfire
on a washer machine	on a chair with no arms
on top of a dryer	against a closed door
on a toilet seat	under the kitchen table
on a rug	on a secluded beach
in a meadow	in front a lit fireplace

Quickies are beneficial because there is not always time to enjoy a full session of love-making.

143

WAYS TO ENHANCE QUICKIES

Occasionally change your location.
Switch you usual roles.
Wear blindfolds to bed.
Slowly massage his erogenous zones.
Fantasize while you're making love.
Let your body feel every part of his body.
Tease each other intensely.
Set up exotic session for one another once each month.
Talk openly about your sexual fantasies with one another.
Have an orgy for two.
Play relaxing sensuous music.
Meet him for lunch in a hotel.

ENVIRONMENTS

I believe that sex can be completely enjoyed at just about any place it happens, but for the sake of safety, respect, legal ramifications and relaxation, I suggest privacy and discretion. A change of pace and routine are sought after qualities which add variety to sex lives. Variety is necessary to keep the home fires burning. Actually the environment is the needed change to add spice to your love-making. Some favorite places as suggested by male friends are: in the embrace of your lovers arms.whenever the mood creates love.

by a campfire or fireplace.
on a boat (water isn't necessary).
by the lake.
on a desk at the office desk.
in a hot tub.
on file cabinets.
on top of a pool table.
on a balcony.
motel at home.
on a golf course.

inside a moving elevator.
in a van.
on top of the car.
on a friends patio.
in the guest bathroom.
on a train.
at the beach.
on bar stool.
in a sauna.

*WHERE NOT TO HAVE SEX:

~in front of children

144

Chapter 29

ORGASMS:

WHAT IT FEELS LIKE

There is much more to intercourse than reaching orgasms. However, women still think that good sex is reaching their orgasm. Coming into "YOUR" full sexual self will be a lot more pleasurable than being sexually who you are not. Once you learn to enjoy your sexuality, your giving and sharing will mean substantially more. Affection, excitement and understanding will expand your sensitivity toward your desires to reach orgasms.

The what, how, and why's of orgasm are not as plain as they seem. Orgasms are the tension release that escalates during sexual arousal and heightened lovemaking. Orgasms are full of temperatures; temperatures of love that are hot and passionate, frigid and cold, warming or cooling. The way people achieve orgasms is reflected in the way they feel.

Sexual pleasures are strengthened by belief in yourself. During the first stages of sexual excitement, the veins in your pelvis, vulva and clitoris dilate and fill up with blood, which in turn makes your sexual area feel full and swollen. As the excitement of sexual tension rises, your body's muscles tense up. You will began to breath faster, your nipples will become harder and as he touches you, your whole body will feel alive and sensitive to his touch.

Stimulation directly and/or around the clitoris with slight pressure on the cervix or other sensitive areas of your body will create the fullness of the pelvic area. This fullness, along with your body's arousal, will build up to an exciting and wonderful peak. To reach beautiful and fulfilling orgasms you should relax and let go of all those tensions that are begging to come out. If you let go, a variation of involuntary and pleasurable contractions will expel blood tissues into your vagina, uterus and rectum. These are the places where waves of sensational stimulations that produce orgasms go. A female orgasm can be felt by the penis because it creates a series of strong vaginal contractions, and her body will sometimes go limp.

Many women say that orgasm feel like a sneeze, hiccup or a long refreshing sigh. It is experienced as slow, fast, sensuous or intense. If a finger, dildo, penis, or vibrator is used on your clitoris or vagina, many different sensations can be experienced. There can also be different sensations if masturbation techniques are used by your lover or your own hands. If you have different lovers, it would naturally feel different with each and sometimes the same lover can make it feel different at different times. Orgasms also feel different as you get older or as your body changes.

ACHIEVEMENT

Some of the best and most successful ways to achieve orgasms vary with the individual trying to achieve the orgasms. From looking at a sensuous man to touching, caressing, massaging, kissing, or deliberate teasing, licking, sucking and penetrations can bring you to orgasms. Some methods work better on some women than others, but all are a matter of personal preference.

For many women, oral sex brings orgasm faster than any other way of making love. And many women agree that its difficult to achieve orgasm with sexual intercourse alone. Women want a multitude of sensations at once. Having sexual intercourse with clitoral stimulation, kissing and caressing all at once usually creates an orgasm. Because of this, a woman prefers to be on top of her partner sometimes because she can control the angle of penetration as well as the clitoral stimulation.

Approximately eleven percent of all women have never had an orgasm. So if you've never felt an orgasm or you aren't reaching it, that doesn't necessarily mean that something is wrong with you or your body. Orgasms are the ultimate pleasure of sex even though sex can be enjoyed without them. Women in general can be orgasmic by masturbating because women know best what it takes to bring their orgasm on.

Just because you don't have multiple orgasms doesn't make you any less a woman. When you began to focus on multiple orgasms, you are getting caught up into quantity rather than quality. Don't you dare feel sexually inadequate if you don't have multiple orgasms. One orgasm per sexual act is as normal and satisfying as none or as multiple orgasm.

Orgasms are important and sex is good for a woman's disposition, complexion and libido. Many lovers haven't come to terms with the female orgasm. Women were told to shut their eyes during sex on their wedding nights. The female orgasm became more and more complicated with every passing year. In the past, whether orgasms were clitoris or vaginal was a big controversy. Women were found to have orgasm after orgasm and this fact put men to shame with their one gun salute. Finding real satisfaction made a big difference to women, even those who are capable of experiencing multiple orgasms found that one was not enough. A woman's lover's job is to help bring her to climax during lovemaking. Working to reach this goal will improve his technique as he practices, benefiting both of you. Insist on your orgasms so that he will know you want satisfaction. Faking can lead to dissatisfaction on the woman's part. It's like crying wolf to him, and it creates frustration and laziness. If you don't let him know he'll feel content and fall asleep without you having a climax.

HELPING HIM TO HELP YOU

Take his hand, and lead it to your clitoris; he'll get the message and start masturbating you. Help to guide his hand to your most desirable spot. Help with the rhythm of his movements by holding his hand as you show him what you like. Talk to him, and let him know what you like, for this is not the time to hold back. If you choose to have an orgasm through oral sex tell him to lick you and rotate your hips in his face as you pull his face, nose and mouth into your vulva. Allow his facial hair to rub against your clitoris.

After your arousal creates an orgasm, tell him what you liked the most make it sound erotic. Wince and sigh with passion. A woman does not have to put up with unsatisfying sex from her husband or lover. Initiative on the woman's part will help the man to understand that you need an orgasm and it's his job as your lover to help you. Having simultaneous orgasms, is more than satisfying to say the least. A woman's orgasm can be triggered by her lover's sperm squirting against her cervix. Men have told me that they experience ejaculation when they feel the quivering and rippling sensations inside a woman's vagina when she comes. If you are in tune with your sensuality, you can experience orgasms easier. Don't be disappointed if you don't experience simultaneous orgasms because it isn't essential. If you don't come, still have fun trying to help your lover to have orgasms. A common female sex problem is failure to have an orgasm. This is not unusual. The three principle reasons are usually easily cured if you...

1. Relax, by letting your body feel at ease.
2. Don't try to hard - it eludes you.
3. Anxiety - The kind that causes a man's penis to flop.

1. Relax, by letting your body go limp. Some experts recommend a drink or maybe a tranquilizer to help you to relax. It's a matter of personal preference. Try not to worry about climaxing. Don't tense up. Be an active participant in your sexual encounter, have fun and think positive

2. Don't try to hard. If your lover doesn't seem to be arousing you. Manipulate his actions by having him put up a little fight for you. He can do this by holding you more, fondling or caressing before you spread your legs for him. Give a little and decline a little, to keep the session interesting and progressive. Say things to him like... kiss my ears, suck my breast. Take control of your sexuality by coming before him and trying to come again with him. Have multiple orgasms so that the both of you will have pleasure.

3. Tolerating sex without orgasm is a matter of preference also. Many women go for years unsatisfied and unfulfilled due to lack of orgasms. Lack of orgasms lead to slow erosion of relationships because the frustrations surface sooner or later in ways detrimental to a relationship.

A sexually happy woman is a sexually sensuous woman. She is also gratified and satisfied. Be a real woman and make sure you're getting your satisfaction. ˙

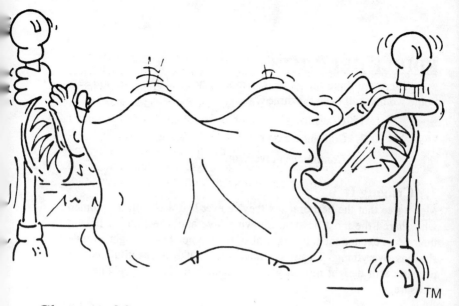

TM

Chapter 30

ORAL SEX:

Many lovers have chosen oral sex to scale them to new heights of sexual excitement. Good oral sex not only excites your partner, it will turn you on when you give it. After a few tries of oral sex any mentally bad tastes will soon disappear.

Many men do not know how to perform cunnilingus correctly. Long tongue strokes are a good beginning. The clitoris is the most sensitive point and it should receive the most attention. It should not be chewed, bitten, or sucked too hard. If your lover has trouble finding it, he should ask for your guidance in finding it. He should ask you how you want it licked, sucked or kissed. If he doesn't ask then you should be woman enough to guide him in the right direction. If he still can't seem to find it, smile into his eyes as you show him. He'll appreciate your participation and openness.

Besides, neither of you will remember any embarrassing questions or moments once you lose yourself into your lovemaking.. The better he becomes in administering oral sex, the more orgasms you will have before intercourse begins.

EDIBLE DELIGHTS

There are three things to remember when indulging in oral sex. Some women call them the three C's.

1. Crave it.
2. Concentrate on it.
3. Continuous movement.

1. Craving It

Men agree that the best oral sex they've ever had was with the women who shared the most passion. Showing love and affection for licking their penis excited them the most also. If a women has the right attitude she has everything. Treating a man's penis like a beautiful tool of pleasure will delight him as well as excite him, therefore giving you pleasure.

2. Concentrate On It

Being able to completely focus on your task without your mind wondering will keep the intensity high.

3. Continuous Movement

Long, continuous and smooth movement with even strokes help the erotic pleasures flow. It also keep the juices flowing. Fast and abrupt movements have been known to decrease passion as well as the flow of love juices. Your vagina can be the central ingredient in a super dessert which can be eaten with gusto. When one lover has fears about fellation or cunnilingus, adding variety to the sexual meal can break down barriers of inhibitions. The vagina can be coupled with many tasty delights. Placing a large towel on the bed can be used to cover your sexual areas. Surprisingly, many couples who began with negative feelings about oral sex try it and find that it becomes part of their regular snack routine. It can also become a part of their nightly bedtime treat. At some point and time your partner will want a blow job, or oral sex. This is nothing more than sucking his penis. This is not foreplay, but a natural part of the sexual act, which also includes orgasms.

As a prelude to sexual intercourse, oral sex is great. It can leads to sexual intercourse. Oral sex can be a prerequisite to sex. In most European nations oral sex is accepted by almost everyone regardless of gender. Many women say that the United States is the blow job champion of the world, I haven't found any statistics to say yes or no to this statement.

Men look for women who are experienced sexually and know how to give a good blow job. Bringing your man to ecstasy with good oral sex will guide him to fulfillment and this should not be considered demeaning.

POINTS TO REMEMBER

Some of the most significant points to remember about oral sex are:

1. Remember to kiss his penis in the same way you would kiss your lover's lips. This type of kissing sensation is erotic and sensuously fulfilling to your lover because it feels as if you are making love to his dick. It sends more passionate overtures to his brain.

2. With practice and patience you will be able to take his penis into your mouth without gagging. Follow these simple steps. Use your hand as an assistant to your mouth. Start off with your mouth wide enough to keep your teeth from accidentally scratching his tender penis skin. Create as much saliva as you can and suck until his penis is thoroughly lubricated. With your hand make a tube bringing your thumb closer to your mouth. Squeeze your little finger around the bottom of his penis shaft, leaving your index finger and thumb loose. Move your hand in an up and down motion in unison with your mouth. Once you've created a tunnel of beef and you're holding it tight, open your mouth as wide as possible, and relax your muscles in your throat. Compress your lips to help create pressure and watch the fireworks begin.

If you get bored it will send messages of unenjoyed dick sucking to your partner. Rest or change your momentum to something else that you'll enjoy. To inflict lasting and pleasurable torment hold his penis shaft and playfully dart your tongue back and forth lightly over the surface of his penis head until he begs for mercy. Some men like to have the underside of their penis sucked. Concentrate on the area directly surrounding his penis hole, because this area is more sensitive to sucking.

Another enjoyable technique is to fill your mouth with hot or cold water and engulf his penis into this sensational pleasure vacuum. Sometimes his penis will be limp But don't let it discourage you, it will soon harden. And for a nice change of pace you can move completely away from his penis and onto his waiting balls. Men love to have their balls licked and gently sucked. For some men their balls have to be sucked and lick-flicked before they consider their blow job completed.

Your tongue forms the most important portion of the mouth because as a blow job perfectionist it is your job to communicate with your partner's penis. The sides, tip, and flat surface of your tongue should be used. As a brilliant conversationalist can turn the conversation to witty, philosophical or emotional, so should you as a master of oral sex.

To accompany your mouth as a part of oral sex, there are several other elements of pleasure. Your hands are a celebrated tool also. They play an active role by stroking, holding and firmly squeezing the shaft of his penis. Many a man likes to have his asshole probed by a finger or two while he's being sucked off. To do this effectively, feel for his anal sphincter muscle; it will help to guide your hand toward the entry for depth. If he doesn't prefer his asshole to be played with he'll slide your hand away. Don't be offended, he's just not ready for this pleasure and he has no idea what he's missing, so be patient with him.

Other men like and prefer to have their neck, nipples, chest, stomach, arms, fingers, legs and toes licked and sucked as a natural part of love-making. Go on and enjoy his entire body. Don't always concentrate on his dick. Don't be surprised if the man of your dreams never says a word or makes any noises during oral sex. He will soon become quite noisy as your technique improves. Don't get upset, just continue to tell him what you want; he'll soon oblige.

Safe sex is a guideline with oral sex also. Use a condom for oral sex, even though transmission of the AIDS virus by oral sex is still debated. If he comes in your mouth, and you didn't use a condom your stomach acids may kill the HIV virus if it's present (see Women and AIDS). Otherwise it's a matter of choice as to whether you spit it out. Rinse your mouth out with a strong mouthwash if this happens during love-making. Some women like to use a mouthwash everytime they indulge in oral sex and some use mouthwash as a common health practice whether their partners climax or not. It's a matter of personal hygiene and preference.

Last, remember that some men can be demanding by trying to pressure you into swallowing his come by telling you it will prove your love. This is only a manipulation tactic to convince you to swallow his semen. Give him a firm NO, and continue to be a REAL WOMAN by not being manipulated into anything that you don't want.

BASIC <u>ORAL-SEX</u> <u>TECHNIQUES</u> <u>TREATS</u>
Lip, Mouth and Tongue Techniques:

When it's time for intimacy, lip, mouth and tongue techniques can be fantastic turn ons. Eating, as many call it, is described as small sucking motions on various parts of the body. Forming the lips in a tight suction is the beginning of erotic feelings that will always be adorned. Once a woman masters lip, mouth and tongue techniques, her man will always feel loved and needed. Your lover will want you to kiss him deeply and meditatively, but give him little nippy bites on his lower lip to bring added arousal. As you lick every square inch of his body from his forehead to his toes concentrate on giving little nips, bites and sucks as you go. When you reach the inner side of his thighs just below his crotch you can start to nibble and lick playfully.

NIBBLE, NIP, LICK, BITE, AND SUCK

<u>Nibbling:</u> To bite with small gentle bites. To nibble you must take small gentle suction type bites with your lips firmly rounded to pull the flesh of your partner within your lips. Many small and lightly forceful nibbles can bring inward pleasures to your partner. Nibble all over his body from his ears down to his ankles and watch the sparks fly. A good sensuous lover keeps her partner slightly and wonderfully off balance. During loving encounters slow and dreamlike biting or a nibble here and there can be the sudden bright idea to set the erotic tone. Some women have had erotic success nibbling continuously on one spot with a prolonged kiss.

<u>Nipping:</u> To pinch. Nipping is similar to nibbling with one exception: to nip you must give little love pecks with the aid of your teeth. You should nip with care and gentleness. Your teeth are used to send deeper sensations than what would be used in nibbling. To nip your lover let your teeth, while slightly closed, slide across your partners flesh. **DO NOT BITE**, if you are trying to nip. It should feel like you are rubbing your own tongue against the surface of your teeth. A good way to practice on nipping is with a peeled banana. Trying not to remove the flesh of the banana from its stalk, use your teeth to lift any debris. The objective is not to leave any impressions on the banana as you clean it. Once you have mastered the banana you can began to nip your partner's penis without fear of hurting him with your nips.

Licking: To bring to a certain condition by passing the tongue over. Licking is just as it's stated "LICKING." There are variations to licking: long strokes, short strokes, sideways, downward, upward and multiple tiny strokes. It's a matter of preference. Whatever it may be, vary to bring more pleasure and excitement to your partner. Practice licking on almost all that you eat. Make it fun as you do it. Don't think of it as work. From licking your own lips with small sensitive strokes to long sensuous strokes. Practice with popsicles, ice cream cones and even links to mention a few. Practice on your drinks by licking the rim without being too obvious. After a few practice sessions you'll find yourself licking your partner to ecstasy. It will become so natural and effortless that you'll do it without noticing.

Practice on your licking skills daily. When you get the licking skills down to a fine art you will possess tongue manipulations that are uncontrollably erotic.

*lick your tongue out as far as it will go and then slowly pull it back in. Do this at least twenty times a day.

*Lick your lover's lips everytime you kiss him. Don't be sloppy or lazy with this one. No one wants to retrieve spit after a kiss. Kisses should be erotic, not sloppy.

*Roll your tongue up, down, in out and from side to side within your lover's mouth.

*Licking the roof of your lover's mouth as you kiss can spark new nerves in a relationship.

*All licks should be continuous, subtle and smooth going. No abrupt stops, always remain fluent and continuous. The best places to lick your partner are: ALL OVER. If you have to stop licking, remember to keep your hands moving until you began to lick again.

Sucking: To draw into the mouth by creating a vacuum with lips, cheeks and tongue. Sucking is more intense than licking, but when applied correctly it may create sensations that your man will request during all love-making sessions. To practice on your sucking techniques, try sucking on things that are listed. Everyone has the power to be a good sucker but in order to become a great sucker you must practice often. You can suck :

*on a popsicle and try not to break the popsicle as you suck. Use your tongue techniques here.

*on bananas or any other foods that desire a sucking motion.

*through straws as often as possible.

*give gentle sucks to your partner's tongue in and out with slow to fast, fast to slow, long, short and searching sucks.
*your partners nipples gently at first then with deeper and stronger force. Pull his nipples all the way in your mouth with sucking motions.
Sucking is a complete turn on when it's done correctly. You mustn't suck too fast or too slow, but with an even rhythm to bring your partner to new heights.

Biting: To feel or to cause sensations. When biting, use gentle bites that slightly press against the surface. Your lover will let you know if you are biting too hard, but try to learn the technique before he screams in pain. Learn to apply the correct amount of pressure on your lover so that he won't develop a negative attitude toward you during love-making.

ORAL SEX GAMES TO PLAY:

1. Use a cough drop the next time you decide to give head to him. Suck on a cough drop for a few seconds to get the mentholatum working in your mouth. The warmth of your breath and the coolness from the cough drop gives his penis a hot and cold effect all at once. It will drive him erotically crazy. You don't have to suck the entire cough drop, about ten to twelve sucks are efficient. Save the best sucking for his penis.
2. Find your favorite lip gloss or flavored taste and add some to the outer sides of your vaginal lips. Don't let him know that you've put it on your vaginal lips because it will take away from the surprise of it all. As he begins to lavish you the added flavor will be an immediate turn on to him and he'll want to eat you until you climax. The sweetness of your new taste will drive him wild. It also adds variety to your vaginal juices and the flavors that you choose will be complimentary to your sex. Buy two to three different flavors so you can change up every now and then. Other additional flavors as suggested by women are:

*whipped cream	*honey
*syrup	*peaches
*chocolate	*wine / champagne / beer
*fruit juices	*powdered sugar
*powdered honey dust (I suggest Kama Sutra Honey Dust)	

Be careful of anything that you put on the vagina or in the vaginal area because this delicate area can be irritated easily.

3 Occasionally, you can treat his penis like a lollipop as you suck on it. Make circles around and around his penis as you go up and down on it. He'll beg for mercy. Caressing his inner thighs, buttocks, anus tummy and other parts of his body that you can reach.

4. Licking his testicles gently as you take them into your mouth can create sensational pleasures for him. Move your tongue up and down, side to side and in slow lavishing licks. This is one of the most erotic pleasures to men and not many women know this one.

5. While giving him oral sex, gently place your finger into his asshole and move it around into to slow and gentle circles.

6. Holding his penis into your mouth and gently shake your head from side to side at the same time. This will send little tingles up and down his spine as well as throughout his penis.

7. Alternating your mouth with your vagina is something that men love. This is called stroke-dipping by women. Men tend to desire this one if the women is open to it.

8. Have your lover get comfortable as he lies on his back. Kneel down beside him and take his penis in the palm of your hand. Run your lips slowly over his penis. Take your tongue and circle his penis head so that it simultaneously wets his penis as well as your own lips. Open your mouth and stretch your lips so that they cover the top and bottom rows of your teeth. Covering your teeth will help to avoid nicks or cutting the foreskin of the penis. The other reason to cover your teeth is to form a smooth firm ridge that creates highly sensitive sensations to the penis. As you form this smooth ridge, place the penis into your mouth down to the base of the penis and then slowly back up the penis head. To keep sufficient lubrication for the penis and to easily slide it in and out of your mouth with ease, wet it a few times with your tongue. Be aware of your speed and sensations are the most fulfilling to him. Remember to get in tune with his body. Study what sensations make him squirm, wiggle or yell out and then concentrate on these sensations. He might like slow, steady, continuous in and out motions or he might prefer strong quick strokes or both. You should know what your man likes. Practice these oral sex manipulations on a regular basis and before you know it, he'll be begging for more.

9. The sprinkle game is very heated up. Sucking at its very best. Sprinkle tiny suction kisses all over his body. Begin from his head and work your way down his entire body, stopping at his toes, then finally coming back up to his penis. Now slip your tongue over all the areas that you just suction kissed, circling his eyes, ears, lips. When you get to his nipples circle faster than you did before like a whirlpool. Pull his nipple into your mouth with suction kisses, pulling as much of his entire breast into your mouth as possible. Knead his nipples and gently pull them again. Suck him with pleasure and enjoyment as if you are trying to suck for taste. Repeat these steps several times over from his head to his toes.

10. The popsicle lick is one of the most sensuous of all. In this one you use your tongue to continuously circle the penis clockwise. As you slide your tongue in and out of your mouth go counter clockwise. To add more thrills and sensations as you slide his penis in and out, up and down go slowly then faster, then slowly again. The ice cream lick has very dramatic effects on your man and it is worth every minute of effort to see the effects of it all. An added joy is to put fresh whipped cream on his penis and really work him over as if you are licking and sucking on your favorite dessert.

11. Teeth make a great prop. Hold your man's penis sideways, like a buttered piece of corn. Slide your teeth up and down his shaft. Giving it a gentle little nip every now and then is fantastic head.

12. Eating fruit can be an added treat when accompanied with good oral sex. Banana's, oranges, berries, cherries, and any other luscious fruits can be eaten as an appetizer to oral sex. Rubbing the juices all over his penis and licking it off will send many sensations all over his body. Trying to keep some of the fruit in your mouth while while sucking his dick is a nice addition also.

13. Mint flavored candies, mouthwashes or breath savers are nice to create cool sensations on his penis. This creates a tangy tongue and mouth that will cause a terrific sensation.

14. As he innocently watches TV. or listens to music, unzip him and suck away to your heart's content.

15. Wake him up with the feelings of your tongue on his penis.

16. Some women feel that a loving and sexy thing to do is to lavish his penile juices after he's had his orgasm. This works well with animalistic sex. It's a fantastic topping on a sexual encounter.

17. Give him gentle kisses on his penis head in a dark restaurant. The fun of it all is sneaking to do it. Make sure the table is dressed in a floor length cloth to provide the appropriate touch of secrecy.

18. Take your man's penis and move it gently between your lips. Hold it with your fingers while pressing its sides with your lips and teeth. Gently pushing his penis a little bit farther into your mouth try to forcefully suck it in and out. Draw it in as far as it will go, pressing the end of his penis against the roof of your mouth. Suck it in deeply as if you are trying to swallow it. He'll experience the deepest ecstasy.

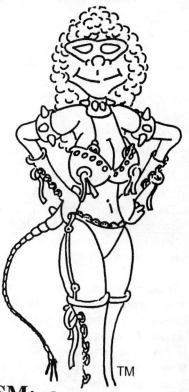

Chapter 31

SADO-MASOCHISM:

SEXUALLY AGGRESSIVE WOMEN

Sexually aggressive women make dancing look like foreplay. She gyrates her pelvis as if it were man-made. Most are confident wearing low-cut clingy tops without bras. Their plan is to seduce their partners. It doesn't have to be a second date. As a matter of fact, it doesn't even have to be a date just as long as she ends her night in erotic pleasures. Sexually aggressive women usually get what they want.

During dinner dates, it's common for the aggressive woman to touch her date on the most private places, in places that aren't typical expressions of affection in public by women. Aggressive women don't exhibit the normal public displays such as: holding hands casually. They do things like, stroking his chest between his shirt buttons or rubbing her toes against his crouch. His face exemplifies the blush that she helps create. These types of women are only with men who satisfy them sexually. They aren't afraid of rejection and their relationships don't take long before initiated sex is reached. They come on strong to men as soon as the first phone call, and they carry condoms confidently. She propositions men with ease and she doesn't hesitate to request needs from her partner. If men aren't ready for her directness, she will dismiss them without the blink of an eye. Being by herself is not a problem because she approves of herself. Some women who are sexually aggressive are motivated by hostility towards men. This unhealthy aggression is used to subconsciously distance themselves from men, by trying to scare men away. In this is fear of abandonment and intimacy. They feel that controlling or intimidating men sexually will emasculate him until he is harmless.

There is healthy aggression also. The female sex drive was very misunderstood until recently. In this chapter, I have focused on many aspects healthy as well as unhealthy. The healthy sexually aggressive woman knows that she is due good sex. She is, in a sense, entitled to good sexual healing. During this period of repression, the sexual revolution has caused many women to come of sexual age. Lust is seldom admitted by most women due to embarrassment. During my interviews with women, they talked about love, marriage and family, but not of craving lustful sex. What I have found out from my research is that most lacked sensuality. Therefore, satisfaction was limited. Women who are healthy aggressors are fueled by their desire to control. Being the aggressor in her eyes is empowering. Having the power to get men to want her is a high, especially if she wants them first. Demanding oral sex (cunnilingus) is usually a sign of the aggressor.

The healthy aggressor is not promiscuous, she just lacks inhibitions. She's a free spirit and wants multiple orgasms. She doesn't have a history of jumping from bed to bed, but when she's with a man whom she's with most of the time, she's monogamous. The aggressive woman displays her body in alluring attire that doesn't look cheap. Her behavior is straightforward utterly. She is independent, proud to be female and she's not sleazy. Aggressive women don't play the normal male attraction games such as flinging hair or playing hard to get.

These women never say no and mean yes. If an aggressive woman does play by the rules, it only lasts a very short while. They rely on their ultra feminine characteristics to attract men. Once the man that she chooses is sleeping with her, she gets completely loose, fondling him, caressing his body parts, initiating sex and introducing her sexual toys with games added. These women create enough excitement to keep from being bored. They find ways to introduce sex into their conversation by saying things like have you read Will The Real Women Please Stand Up views on orgasms. Friendly touching is a sign of availability used by these women. She will not get overly aggressive unless she sees passion in his eyes.

AGGRESSIVE DESIRES:

Healthy aggressive women will never feel a need to hide their desires. If she wants to be touched on her vagina she'll say so. Her voice and requests turn him on. Asking politely and sensuously can help to initiate other forms of pleasure. Sex is joyful and men love the unbridled passion. Going after her own pleasure is the positive attribute of the aggressive woman. Men feel less pressure when woman go after their own orgasm. Putting his needs first won't make you a better lover, but pursuing personal satisfaction rates the highest when making love.

If you're afraid of rejection, play by the old rules of seduction, until romance develops. Some men are scared of take charge women. Men want the first time to be their idea, so play the game until you get what you want sexually. Some men may never reveal that a come-on by a woman makes them feel uncomfortable. Performance anxiety can set in if a woman takes the lead. A man can even lose his erection if a woman is too pushy. Remember to take it slowly until he trusts you. When you're sure he's safe, let it all loose and make safe love.

RULES FOR AGGRESSIVENESS

1. Assuring your own satisfaction is not wrong or selfish.

2. Tell him politely the graphic details of what you want even if you have to read it to him from a book.

3. Don't get angry if he doesn't offer what you crave. Don't confuse table manners with bedroom manners.

4. When he touches you be sure to respond by asking for more if that's what you want.

5. Initiate sex once you sense he's comfortable.

6. Don't feel guilty when asking for more sex if you need it. He'll ask if he needs it.

7. Don't allow good loving to get too serious. Remember to keep it fun.

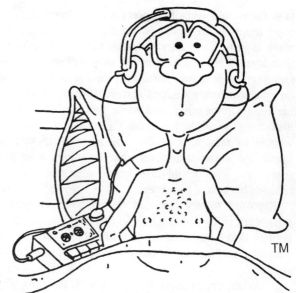

TM

Chapter 32

SEX TALK:

CONVERSATIONS

Conversations consist of not only what you say, but how you say it. The more accomplished the conversationalist, the more she makes use of tone, facial expressions and variation of gestures for emphasis, thought, wit, and empathy for expertise.

Sex talk is not a single exclamation of moans, groans, and squeals until finally-ejaculation. Sensuous and erotic turn on's can be interpreted in many different ways. Sex talk is in the ears of the receiver. It creates and describes probably one of the most potent means for changing direct sex into an inviting adventure.

Noise can be associated with sex whether good, bad, pleasurable or painful. Most women still feel inhibited or even foolish when verbal during love-making because of its unfeminine like characteristics. Women sometimes don't want men to recognize the fact that they are enjoying themselves.

If a woman wants to make sounds as a natural to sexual pleasure, then she should verbally express it to her lover. As a woman becomes more aroused, her heart and breath rates speed up. As she begins to reach orgasm these rates speed up actually three to four times faster than normal. No real woman can keep still when all that excitement is going on inside of her. Some men I interviewed were genuinely turned on by a woman's sounds of ecstasy. It made him feel like the king of her night. On the other hand, some men felt like noise was a turn off or distracting to their love-making. One of the most important things for a woman to remember is that she must be in tune with her own sensuality. She must discover what she enjoys in sex as she accepts her sensuality. She should also know what noise making antics will enhance her sexual pleasures.

Exposure to sex talk can be positive, rewarding and quite an experience if it's with a man you love and adore. The first response to sex talk is to be shocked or offended. Some women are even turned off immediately. The biggest complaint by most women is they feel cheap and dirty.

Loosening up, relaxing and going with the flow will initially seem crude and disgusting, but you'll shortly find yourself being turned on by sex talk in a sensuous way. Explicit sex talk can turn you on if you refuse to get caught up in the nice girl syndrome. As he says one thing, mentally reverse it to your positive thoughts. For example if he says "Suck my dick baby," then you'll say to him "I love the way you turn me on." Then, one night when you're making love, get immersed in the sensuous thought of it all and let your private thoughts become a matter of public arousal between the two of you. After doing this a few times you won't be embarrassed to verbalize your feelings.

If you find that sex talk is not for you, then seductively verbalize your feelings by saying simple things like, "ummmmmmm, I like that" or "ummmm I needed that." It will give the practice you need without talking dirty. As you make love, practice verbalizing your desires and feelings, so that you can communicate with your lover in an erotic way. Another good start to sex talk is to verbally tell your lover what you want, how you want it and whether or not it feels good during your love-making.

VOICE TONE

Nothing is more erosive than a irritating voice when making love to the man you love. No man wants to hear a fingernail scratching voice when he's holding you close in the heat of passion. Many women practice on improving their voices by listening to themselves on tape recorders or dictaphones. Don't sound like you have laryngitis to your lover. That can be very unsexy and unromantic. Don't spend all your time and money making yourself beautiful and then when he hears your voice, he's turned off completely. Some voice improvement techniques are:

**take a deep breath and hold for approximately eight seconds as you answer the phone. Let your breath out slowly as you speak. It adds to the sensuality of your voice. Continue to do this technique while holding your breath until it's natural, fluent and pleasant.

**soften your tone by lowering your voice everytime you speak. Women with loud, boisterous voices are a turn off. Begin now, and notice how provocative you've become.

**practice on your pronunciation and correct word usage. To have a beautiful speaking voice and good pronunciation are double threats to any man of class. Remember, romancing your man, is the goal, not discouraging him.

A good point to remember about voice quality is to think, act and talk sensuously. Talk with sensuality and believe that you are sensuous with all your will. If you believe in sensuality, you will become the more sensuous person that you've always wanted to be. Work on improving your voice tone by practicing each day. Your voice should not be abrasive or harsh. Remember to also use words that compel you to make sexy sounds with their pronunciation.

Some words that encourage provocative sounds are words that begin with the letter "S". I've listed few: suck, sucked, sucking, sex, sexy, sensuous, sensual, sequence, seduction, seep, semaphore. To find more sensuous "S" words, look in the index of this book or the dictionary. They have many "S" words that can help to build your sensuous vocabulary.

Use your speech organs to produce provocative sounds when you are speaking to your lover. A sweet, soft, sexy voice will lure any willing man in your direction if you are willing to put forth the needed effort. Look at it this way, men want to be needed and men need to be wanted. It's up to you as a woman to make your man feel that he's needed, just as it is his responsibility to make you feel needed. Imagine all that can be accomplished when you say the right things in the right way in the correct tone to him.

TELEPHONE SAVVY

Giving good phone sex is very necessary to keep a relationship steamy. Using your imagination to make him feel good about himself helps to build his ego. Having good phone savvy keeps many men interested as well as happy. Seduce your lover by calling him on the telephone and saying erotic and sexy things. Assure him that you miss him and tell him that he won't regret your time together.

Even Ma Bell has ventured into the phone sex business. Many newspapers and magazine have advertisements that feature sexy women with large breasts or male hunks with large penises encouraging you to phone in for a dollar or two per minute. They actually make you believe that you are the caller they've been longing to hear. Thousands of men and women call everyday for two main reasons: Some want to masturbate as they listen and others want to meet women or men.

Masturbation over the phone has advantages over real life. Some obvious reasons are: you don't have to dress for the occasions and the threats of unsafe sex are not present. Phone sex is not threatening to the listener either, because face to face rejection doesn't exist. There's always someone to talk to. People calling for phone sex can use their imaginations to the limit without embarrassment or belittlement.

Experiencing phone sex can teach you about many aspects of sex that you've never thought about before. Exaggeration is quite natural on the telephone. Even though there are professional phone sex lines we will deal with your personal phone line as phone sex to your lover. To make it interesting to the both of you here are some suggestions:

Your overall attitude is important. To turn your lover on with phone sex you should sound like a person who is genuinely interested in the phone conversation. Be as verbal as you possibly can. As you talk to him use a lot of adjectives describing yourself and your favorite sexual encounter with him. If you haven't had the pleasure of a sexual encounter with him yet, describe yourself and what you would like to do to him. Your description should help your man to think of an image. Use your sexiest sounding voice. Practice by using a hushed-low sexy voice. Making sounds of climaxing will give vivid images to your partner. Coming over the phone usually lasts longer over the phone than it does in real life. Don't fall into the trap of using the phone as a way to avoid intimacy or to avoid a real relationship. The trials and tribulations involved in knowing how to use phone sex are just for entertainment and are not a replacement for kissing, cuddling or a real live beating heart.

SENSUOUS CASSETTES

Making a Sex Cassette

1. Practice on your cassette to find your sexiest voice tone.
2. Call a phone sex line and learn the do's and don'ts of phone sex. This will help you to learn what works.
3. Remain mentally seductive by having a gentle introduction, slow build up and soft resolution.
4. Choose his favorite song as your background music. Make sure it relates to the two of you.
5. Don't use any other provocative female sounds or moans.
6. Choose a song that he won't sing or hum along with...something romantic and seductive.
7. Music should be subtle and low in the background.
8. Choose a long playing song that makes you feel romantic and open.
9. Choose a comfortable, uninterrupted environment. Turn the ringer off on your phone.
10. Begin your tape with your sexiest hello, but don't let it sound rehearsed. Use his name or the nick name that you gave him, and tell him in detail about sexy thoughts that you've had about the two of you.
11. Choose sexy clothing, but take them off before taping and go naked. Taking them off heightens your romantic mood.
12. While you're thinking of him and as you began to masturbate, tell him what you're doing as you do it.
13. Be as true and as honest as possible. Intently intensify... no faking.
14. Rest for at least an hour after you complete your tape.
15. The next day listen to it and if you decide to mail it to him, send it along with a erotic note to him. One day mail services are quite nice.
16. One day mail services are quite nice.
17. Put it in his lunch box... or slip it into his car audio cassette deck.

Now sit back, relax and wait on his call. Once you get his call, play out one of your favorite fantasies and don't forget to sound as provocative over the phone as you did on the cassette.

NOISY TURN ON'S

Women prefer to be joyously noisy in their beds, but they have been afraid that they'll make the wrong noise, say the wrong things and eventually turn their men off. The fact is that most men want you to be expressive and uninhibited. They don't mind if you sound provocative or expressively mellow. Basically any sounds that you make will turn your man on. Noise is an indication that your lover is turning you on, which is what most men adore. He wants to know that he's giving you what you want. Noises make him wild because most men interpret noises as kinky. They believe that they are turning you on when you make noises.

Foreign words are known to drive men wild during sex, if hearing English is all their use to. Foreign words are thought of as sensuous during sex.

Men aren't mind readers, that's why they like to be told things in bed. Telling your man that he looks good, that he smells good or that he's good in bed are forms of sex talk that men appreciate. Other things that he likes to be told are, that his eyes are gorgeous, his eyelashes turn you on, his skin feels fantastic and other complimentary things about his body will please him.

Another male sex talk tactic is to ask sensuous questions. A man feels desirable and important in bed when a woman whispers sweet nothings in his ear during love-making. Some sensuous questions might be "Can you put that inside of my vagina", "What are you going to do to me?", "Can I taste you?", "Will you taste me?". Try to think of your own sex questions to ask him during love-making and watch him get turned on more.

You can also start off by describing what you're doing or going to do sexually to your lover. Men love this. As you move forward, put more sensuous feelings into your words. As the intensity heightens your partner will squeal in delight and also say a few words himself!

NOISE AFTER SEX

When it comes to sexual performance, men are basically puppy dogs who are taught only a few new tricks. After they're finished, the responses that they really want to hear is Good Boy, for the good sex. Since vocalizing is natural after sex, go ahead and sound off. Don't think about the negatives and please don't worry about it. Get in bed with your man and say what feels good to you. You'll find that the things you say will be just what he wanted to hear. Being creatures whose lives are sometimes captured by a net of words, they heighten our excitement as we perform sexually. Sex talk creates a potent means of straightforward sex into something more erotic for men as well as women. For many men, going to bed with a woman who has enough eroticism to talk dirty is a turn on in itself.

Vocalizing should come natural to you since you've been doing it ever since you were a baby. Whether you're using words or just making provocative noise gets you back into that erotically innocent state. Don't over prepare, or think too much and for your sake don't worry. When you're with your man, let your erotic vocal cords take over. You'll be surprised and pleased with what comes out of your mouth. You'll find that you'll know exactly what to say.

Enjoy playtime.

TM

Chapter 33

TURNING HIM ON

EROTICA

To achieve intense pleasures in sex, more sensuous contact has to be made by lovers. It can sometimes become difficult for a woman to release her inhibitions and enjoy the pleasures involved with being a woman. Turning him on as well as yourself will help with ridding sexual hang ups. Women feel more comfortable in their relationship as they begin to express love. Mood and privacy are the basic concerns of women when making love. Rediscover your erotica and make love more satisfying for the two of you. Some women manage to keep their sensuality in full bloom long after their friends have thrown in the towel. Staying in tune with your sensuality and your sexuality can help you to maintain heightened desire as you continue to make good love. If you've suddenly lost interest in making love and you can't seem to get the hots for your lover, you have a headache, you're focused on the bills, or other non sexual activities, you need to rediscover your self and get turned back on. Being sexually in tune, alive and vibrant is vital to your relationship. Women who have lost the desire or the drive to have sex are growing old before their time. Loss of sexual appetite leads to frustrated women and the possible loss of your man. When you suddenly lose the desire to make love or your interest in sex, you should get in touch with your own body. If you put out undesirable messages, the man in your life begins to think that he is undesirable, unloved and unwanted.

KEEPING HIM TURNED ON

Here are some suggested ways to keep your lover turned on.
1. Sit close and touch him sensuously as often as possible.
2. When standing next to him stroke his back with one of your hands, remembering to move your hand slowly and sensuously.
3. When at social gatherings brush your nipples across his back each time you pass him.
4. Pull him closer as you kiss him, don't let him be the aggressor all the time. He'll love it.
5. Give long, lingering, and playful kisses.
6. Make him feel that you like to kiss him by giving lots of tongue kisses.
7. Glide your hips toward him as you kiss him and roll onto his penis sensuously.
8. With all your clothes on straddle him and kiss him passionately sometimes.
9. Play with his nipples each time you kiss him.
10. Do all the things that he likes.
11. Blindfold him and make love to him. Tell him no peeking.
12. Blindfold him and give him head for at least an hour.
13. Become willing to share your sensuous ideas with him.
14. Look him directly into his eyes as you jack him off.
15. Look him directly into his eyes as you masturbate yourself.
16. Prepare his favorite meal, and name a new dessert after his penis.
17. Excuse yourself from his presence insert your forefinger into your vagina, return to him and as you hug him give him a long sensuous kiss. Then slowly glide your scented finger seductively under his nose.
18. As you stare into his eyes, slowly and seductively suck on an icecube. Move the ice cube in and out of your mouth with your tongue. As you release it from your sensuous lips, lick the rim of your glass slowly and sensuously.

19. Have him massage your clitoris with his penis as a part of foreplay.
20. Wear something sexy to bed at least five days out of the week.
21. Buy a garter belt and wear it with no panties, and as he eats dinner open and close your legs so that he can see your hungry vagina.
22. Revamp by buying sexy matching bra and panty sets.
23. Buy a vibrator and learn how to use it on yourself and then teach him how to use it on you.
24. Buy sheer stocking instead of support hose.
25. Wear laced bras regularly.
26. Read sexual books to liven up your sensuous thinking.
27. Give good phone sex. Talk sweet nothings on the phone and don't forget to coo and ahh a lot. Seduce your man by making a sensuous call to him for a date.
28. Hire him for an evening of passionate sex. Tell him that you're going to pay him a hundred dollars an hour. He'll be thinking about it all day.
29. Look good when your man gets home from work. He probably sees beautiful women daily, some who probably flirt with him. Don't give him a reason to have an affair.
30. Tell him that he turns you on and mean it.
31. Be a good listener when he talks to you, look him directly in eyes and listen to what he has to say.
32. See it in your heart to give him his fantasy.
33. Work to be the best sexual partner he's ever had.
34. Think about sex with your lover on a regular basis. The more you think about it, the sexier you'll become.
35. Schedule two fantasy dates per month. He's responsible for one and you're responsible for the other one. Keep all plans secret from each other. Plan an evening around the fantasy. It can be as wild as you want. The trick is to make it a date to remember.
36. While giving oral sex take a piece of ice into your mouth. As you slip his penis into your mouth, rotate the ice cube all around his penis. Be sure to suck, lick and massage his penis with your tongue until he begs you to stop. This technique is very beneficial to a wimp penis or one that has gone asleep before its time.
37. Place his penis into a glass of champagne and slowly lick the champagne off. Stick his penis in the glass again and this time take a drink from the glass and began to suck his dick. The bubbles of the champagne plus your sucking action will create new sensations that will give him goose bumps as his knees weaken.

38. Tie your lover to the bed and tease him over and over again. The active lover waits until the passive lover is tied up before she takes her clothes off. Once she ties him up she seduces him with her actions. She touches him with parts of her body only. After seductively stripping for him, kiss him all over his body, remembering not to miss a single spot. Alternate soft to firm touches on his body. This will naturally drive him wild. As he squirms and twitches about, leave him there and get a drink or find something else to do for about two minutes. These two minutes that you're away will feel like twenty to him. Once you get back, start the process over again beginning with light kisses all over his body.

39. Send items of clothing to your lover. Send him one piece at a time on a weekly basis. These items of clothing can extend or lengthen your time for as long as you want it to. For example, if you want him to receive all items in one week, send everything at once. If you want the time to spread out into two weeks send half this week and half on the following week. If you want to drag it out longer select the order that you want to send the pieces of clothing and stretch it out until you're ready to be fitted by your lover. This game can be as sensuous and erotic as you want it to be, or as subtle as you want. These pieces of clothing should be sensuous and erotic. Once he's received a complete outfit allow him to dress you so that later that evening he'll be able to also undress you.

Chapter 34

LOVE ™·

Romance is thought to be made in heaven, but real love often begins long after sexual passions have cooled and fantasies have ended. A woman must give herself to love-making with real enthusiasm. Love is the sharing of self that makes a woman whole. Love gives a woman her existence and a sense of purpose. Women who respect love, and revel in love, should learn to understand it. You can enjoy life and yourself without love and be physically satisfied, but only with love can you be fulfilled. Imagine that you are in a relationship that's full of hope and positive vibes. You feel good about yourself with this person. Your self-esteem is high, you're having fun, you feel the heat when you're with him and you enjoy the intimacy. Just the two of you, and love.

<u>FALLING</u> <u>IN</u> <u>LOVE</u>

Many significant factors contribute to falling in love. Though these factors vary in numbers as well as in levels of emotions, women have told me their ways of knowing when they're in love.

Women are in love when :

~you think his childish ways are endearing.

~y our ways have become more spiritual, generous and sympathetic.

~you began to buy lacy lingerie to show your stuff.

~you began to subscribe to sports magazines just for him.

~you adjust to his lifestyles.

~you began to say the word " we" more.

~you send love letters for no reason at all.

~you listen to every word in love songs.

~you spend an afternoon of golf, following him instead of playing?

~you only call your friends when he's out of town.

~you began to forget your priorities.

~you get rid of old gifts from old lovers.

~you forget to eat because you thought of him.

~you lose weight without trying.

~you allow him to choose your new hair style.

~you wear the dress you hate, just because he bought it.

~you feel that he can do no wrong.

~you stop fantasizing about other men.

~you think he's adorable when he buys you tools for your birthday.

~you blame your girlfriend when he flirts with her.

~you keep score during his favorite football game.

~you give up sweets.

~you live in and out of your car due to stay overs.

~you think his bald head is sexy.

~you forget he's bald headed.

~you think his sweat smells sexy.

~you shave under your arms and legs daily.

~you try to kiss up to his mother even when you dislike her.

~you give him pet names or nick names.

~you see him and your panties get wet.

~you see him and your vagina throbs

~you see someone who looks like him and your heart begins to flutter.

~you call his mother for no reason at all.

~you forget that he's a slob.

~you ignore his snores in bed.

~you thinks he's exciting while he sleeps.

~you laugh at his dull jokes.

~you forgive him for having an affair.

~you buy his Christmas gift in June.
~you let him drive your car even though he won't let you drive his.
~you try to please him too often.
~you compete against his ex-girlfriend or ex-wife.
~you massage his feet even though he has athlete's foot fungus.
~you kiss him even though his breath stinks.
~you don't notice the large fluid filled bumps on his face.
~you rearrange your closets and drawers to make room for him.
~you tell all your close friends not to call.
~you are more happy with him than you are with yourself.
~you respect him more than you respect yourself.
~you suck in your stomach when he's around so that he won't notice your fat.
~you think that his animal mannerisms are sexy.
~you know that he doesn't make good love, but you convince yourself that it's good.
~you no longer crave your favorite foods, you crave his.
~you don't take a bath right away after sex, because you want his scent to linger a little longer on you.
~you try to keep your panties that are your period panties hidden so that he won't think you're a slob.
~you ignore the fact that his feet stink.
~you put love notes in his lunch box.
~you ignore his lies to you.
~you change your religious preference to his.
~you think he's too helpless to shop for groceries.
~you believe that you're overweight, just because he says so.

OBSESSIVE LOVE

In the beginning it's not always obvious that a relationship will become troubled and painful. Many couples say that initially their relationship was the origin of great happiness. Many couples recall the lusty glorious sex they enjoyed. They recall the best friend syndrome that they felt when talking to their partners. Sex was an unexplainable high. With very sexual and constant approaches to love-making, a relationship that, at first, seemed to have high hopes, can soon turn frustrating and painful.

Women who experienced obsessive love felt as though they had lost total control of their lives. Their relationships that became obsessive usually ended with great difficulty and sorrow. It's a story that many women are familiar with. As these women broke free from these obsessive relationships, they began to help themselves as well as others.

Some of the characteristics that presented frustrations to women who have dealt with obsessive love are:

.wasting years of their lives with men who didn't care for them.

.long hard and strenuous road to recovery.

.having frustrated long-term affairs with married men.

.experiencing emotional or physical abuse.

Women over the years have shown courage in finally breaking free of obsessive love. Writing down details of their pain is an avenue to healing. Obsessive love rarely ends happily, but it's noted for identifying symptoms of destructive relationships and about healing from the stress and pain of obsessive love.

AN OBSESSIVE PICTURE:

Not every woman experienced their relationship as satisfying and fulfilling at the beginning. Many women say that they experienced trouble from the very start. They felt frustrated, sad and yearned for a fulfilling relationship. They became so hooked that they could not stop thinking of the man. In the midst of these affairs they were drained of energy and their lives became difficult to live. The obsessive relationship became critical and very insulting and self-esteem dipped to an all-time low. Women also felt that it was their duty to make the relationship work. (See Things Women Fear) Many lovers were so attached that they couldn't walk away from the pain that they were experiencing. This same group felt that he needed her to survive. Waiting and hoping to see a change in him kept many women holding on. They said that their lovers would give enough attention to let them know that he was interested. However, he would be so inconsistent that hopes would shatter.

When a goal is too easy or too difficult we tend to give up. When the presence of small, positive feedback is present, we stay to fight. We may not even be getting enough from it, yet, we stay. Some women say that they went to great lengths to avoid this obsessive love but somehow he would always find her. Some women said that they felt completely different, uninhibited and satisfied when they were with him. He made them feel sensuous and sexy.

DARK OBSESSION

The continuous pain of love and the inability to end it for good to a woman who was not capable of respectful relationships brought emotional abuse and sometimes physical abuse. Women in these relationships are not only beaten, but they are the beaters. If they are on drugs and their addiction escalates, so does the violence and abuse. While experiencing dark obsession, if a woman felt that he didn't care she might try suicide and then call him to tell him about it.

BREAKING THE CYCLE

When a person finally decides to leave a painful relationship, it won't be easy, but it is possible if the person is ready and/or gets help. Powerful inner strength was reported to be found. Many also found undying strength in religion. Women who had experienced obsessive love found that breaking free was an uphill struggle. For some women, trying to forget him was more difficult than they thought possible. The physical separations were not enough.

Many women suggested innovative ways to help get over an obsessive love. Some women found help from their churches. Self-esteem was regained in the church. Some women visited a close friend to regain identity. After all the trying and waiting on him to change, many women finally realized that he could never give her what she wanted. Many women benefited from obtaining counseling and using the twelve step program. They began to understand and learn from their mistakes. Learning how not to repeat these mistakes was a major challenge. One of the books that I found to be a great help to women was <u>Women Who Love Too Much</u> by Robin Norwood. If an unhappy affair has you by the throat and you still want it, you are a victim of obsessive love. These are some of the tips suggested to help you soften the blow until you can get help.

1. **Give Yourself Some Space.** When you're in an abusive relationship, it's usually because you stop voicing your opinion and you began to deny your needs. Then began to doubt your ability to see the situation clearly.

2. **Trust Yourself.** After you make a clear decision, trust your judgment. Making some wrong turns can later help you to make the right decisions. The key is to trust yourself; believe that you can and will make the right decisions and this will help you to move forward.

3. **Set Small Goals.** Finding a better life often requires planning. Write a wish list naming everything that you want. Write long and short-term goals. Decide what steps to take to reach your goals. Break each goal into steps so that they are manageable. Work toward them day by day.

4. **Figure Out Why You Loved.** Make a list of all the traits that you want in a lover. What you'll end up with is your missing self, the person who you wish that you could be. In an addictive state, you'll forget the person within you. Our love affairs offer potential to grow personally, when in the addictive state.

5. **Uncover the Real Issues.** When you're depressed over a troubled love affair, it helps to step away from the experience and take a look at your life. To examine what is going on in the present the good and bad elements will help you to see a clearer picture. Ask yourself what makes you satisfied and happy versus uncomfortable and unhappy. Write it out on lists also. Examine your past the same way. Writing about your life is an invaluable tool for understanding the patterns in your struggles with yourself and others. Many feel that insight was gained from their relationships. This, in he long run, helped in their personal growth. Many women felt that their experiences have helped them in both good and bad ways. Thus, new insights, awareness and a greater inner strength and confidence were developed. Many moved on from their obsessive relationships to enjoy healthy, stable, and satisfying relationships with their man.

LASTING LOVE: KEEPING LOVE ALIVE

Lasting love takes two. While nothing last forever, there are certain things that women can do to help their love remain strong and be fun. Women who have been in relationships for five years or more were interviewed for this section. What I realized as we talked was that it was not the quantity of gifts, money or material items that helped their relationships survive...it was lessons learned together.

BEAUTIFUL <u>LESSONS</u> TO REMEMBER:
1. **Perform rituals of love.**
   Rituals are necessary to keep love alive and interesting. Some common love rituals are:
   .help to keep each other safe, secure and warm at all times.
   .if one of you takes a briefcase to work, the other writes a love note and slips it in the briefcase.
   .if one of you goes away overnight, he or she leaves a love note on the pillow.
   .if one has to work on a Sunday, the other brings the newspaper, goes along for company and remains quiet.
   .even if busy, the other stops to call during the day.
   .hold onto each other for one minute without a sound during these imes of the day...mornings, evenings, when nervous, when company leaves.
   .if watching television, stop for a moment to hug the other one.
   .sleep together and curl up together like spoons.
   .allow and give regular touching.
   .the one who is angry makes up, by telling a "Once Upon A Time Story."
2. **Tell him how wonderful he is.**
   Tell him how much you love him, how happy he makes you, how much you enjoy spending time with him. Get in the habit of stroking his ego and do it regularly and for no reason at all. Try to love the part of him that is the least perfect and before you know it you will.
3. **Marry your best friend.**
   No matter how old the relationship or the marriage is, continue to talk with one another. A man can be your best friend if you give him half a chance, but many women feel that men are looking for passion instead of friendship. It's said that there is nothing more passionate than friendship. As fast as the world is moving and changing, there are many things to talk about. If you marry your best friend, the talk never grows old, the sex never grows old.
4. **Never purposely hurt feelings.**
   Learn to express your frustrations and voice your anger without aiming for the jugular. Cruel words can't be taken back or forgotten. Be careful because strength can't be gained by lashing out with unkind words. Whatever you say harsh will work on both of you because it takes both of you to keep this boat afloat.

5. Keep your intimacy a mystery.
Closeness enriches your marriage. To attain intimacy in your lives here a few suggestions:
.learn to enjoy each other's togetherness, even when doing different things.
.wake up early enough to put in time for horseplay and breakfast together.
.wake each other up for good-by kisses when going away on business trips or out of town.
.respect each other, try wearing clothes and scents that both of you like.
.continue to play games and court with one another.
.cherish your times in solitude together. Revel in your privacy.

6. Remember to keep the passion burning.
If you want to keep your love alive, you won't wait around for sudden moods of passion to strike. Great sex needs play, which is different from traditional foreplay. Playing stimulates your sexual appetite. By playing you can set the stage for preplanned love-making later. Make your own magic, don't wait on it to come to you.

REASONS TO MAKE LOVE

If you're finding it a problem to make love with your man, stop making excuses and find a reason!!! Has it been weeks, months, or maybe even years? Okay you're a little busy with the kids, the job, your own career or just overextended on just about everything. So what? Putting sex last is a little selfish on your part. Oh, you say you've forgotten how to have sex...so it's been that long. To make love tonight or any night should be fun, so to help you out I've listed some seductive reasons that are just as much fun as making love.

Reason #1   You want to make love:
Making love at anytime for more than thirty minutes will help to burn off those calories that you're struggling to get rid of.

Reason #2   Breakfast Snack:
For that early morning love session...rename it breakfast. Everytime he asks for breakfast, give him sex. Tell him having him for breakfast makes you hungry for him.

Reason #3   Brunch:
For that middle of the day love session...rename it brunch. As a light

snack, give him head until he comes.

Reason #4 Dinner:
For a late night love feast...call it a late night snack and have him eat YOU until YOU come.

Reason #5 Your dinner date was canceled:
Have him get dressed to go out, but serve him a romantic dinner for two at home with candle lights and the whole bit. Then strip him of all clothing and make love on the kitchen table.

Reason #6 You'd like to play sex tennis:
Reserve a day to play tennis and tell him that the only balls you'll need are his nuts. Then cancel the game and make love wild, passionate love.

Reason #7 You have a special gift for him:
Tell him that you have something special for him and give him only two guesses to figure out what it is. If he doesn't guess what it, is he has to give you head. If he guesses it by the second try you have to give him head.

Reason #8 You want to feel the fire:
Gasping, panting and screaming are required in this reason to make love. Besides it won't hurt the sound system.

Reason #9 You need practice:
Tell him that you've found this new game to play and the more you practice the better you'll get at it. He'll want to play more often if you use your sensuous imagination in the bedroom.

Reason # 10 You need sleep:
Have a wild, passionate loves session to sleep more peacefully. He'll understand after you tell him why it's his duty to help you go to sleep. Afterwards fall asleep sensuously in his arms.

Reason #11 There's nothing sensuous showing at the movies:
Tell him that you'd like to make your own movie with him as your star, even though we already know he's just the co-star.

Reason #12 You want to give him a sensuous back rub:
As you sensuously rub his back, slide your breasts, buttocks and vagina all over his body. The stimulation from the heat that your body will create will bring sensuous allure to his back rub.

Reason #13 You haven't been sensuous lately:
Let him know while you're making love that now you see things a little bit clearer. Be sure to mention that if he keeps it up you'll be able to regain your senses before he knows it. As you begin to come, whisper or yell out loud (it's up to you how loud you'll say it) that "I love what you do to me.", or., "I like the way you make me feel"., or add your own to make it more personal.

Reason #14   You need some sensuous therapy:
When he asks what can he do to make you feel better, suggest skinny dipping in the sauna, pool, shower or tub. You can make it as fun and sexy as you want. One good thing to remember is if you're dipping in the bathtub, make the water warm, add your favorite scents, get in and relax with him.

Reason #15   You're cold:
Tell him that making passionate love will lower the wind chill factor by at least sixty percent.

Reason # 16   You can make the earth move:
Bet him two hours of head that you can make love to him and cause the earth to move.

Reason # 17   You want to thank him for washing your hair last night:
Reward him with a romantic picnic at your favorite park or lounge area.

Reason #18   Tell him that you know a winning lottery number:
Add the number of climaxes that you and your lover experience in one week. Multiply this number by the size of your bed in inches. Once you hit the lottery run out and buy WILL THE REAL WOMEN PLEASE STAND UP.

Reason #19 You want to discover the lost erogenous zone:
Make plans to be the first to climax. If he climaxes before you, you owe him more sensuous sex. DON'T CHEAT!

Reason # 20   Your sensuous fortune cookie told you to do it:
Make up your own sensuous fortunes and place them wrapped on a spoon or fork handle each time you serve him a meal. He should read his fortune and follow the directions and then you read yours and follow the directions also.

Reason #21   I decided not to do the laundry:
Instead of doing the laundry, make passionate love to him.

MAKING LOVE BETTER

Remember when you used to leap into each other's arms after only a few hours apart. The only thing that gets turned on now is the television. Sexual excitement has always been associated with naughtiness, badness, or dirtiness. All these elements are soon lost in sex that's too serious. When couples become committed to one another often times sex soon becomes a job. What was once fun to do, now becomes a hassles to enjoy. Something that you once liked to do has now become something that you're supposed to do.

Remember the joyous QUICKIE? Sexual enjoyment begins and ends with excitement, imagination and playfulness. It means returning to the attitude that sex is fun, not a chore or a serious business governed by rules and other people's habits. Adopting an attitude of anything goes and what goes on tonight might not go on the next time can improve your love life. Allow yourselves to mix up the places where you have sex: in the bathroom, in the shower, in the living room. It's really up to you. Let your imagination soar. (see Sexual Intercourse Chapter 28)

FALLING OUT OF LOVE

One of the unpleasant facts of life is falling out of love. Some women do find it difficult to fall out of love. Despite all the mistreatment by men to them or the insecurities of their own, there is the possibilities of being the fool. In most cases, you should be able to let by gones be gone. But what if he's the only man you want, the only man you feel that you need, and you've got your nose wide open to him. To rid yourself of this relationship, when you've had enough but can't let go, follow these simple steps:

1.   List all your positive qualities on a poster board and post them on your mirror, in front of your toilet, or any place that you can see the list more than once a day.
2.   Run a nice morning bath and close your eyes as you soak. Think of all the positive attributes that you have and smile. Smile at the beginning of your new life.
3.   As you step out of the tub, say his name once and when you say it use a belittling word to rhyme with his name such as: Dam you Sam, Spoiled Carl. Be as unaffectionate as you can when you say his name. Mean what you say and say what you mean.
4.   Write his name on a piece of paper. Gather up all the memorabilia that you have of him shaving creams, pictures, colognes and put them all in a bag and dump them in the trash. Remember that trash belongs in the trash.
5.   Take cards, letters or any writings and tear them up into small pieces. One by one toss the pieces in the toilet, in trash can, the trash compactor, and recite his name as negatively as you can. You are allowed to curse as you rid yourself of him. Good. Now, you've thrown away the emotional tie that you have to him.

6. Go out and buy a sexy new outfit and began partying again, but don't pick out a man on the rebound. You can date, but don't fall in love too quickly again or you'll be repeating these rituals again.

7. Don't look for a duplicate of the man you just split up with. Don't look for one with his features, build or habits. Starting over means just that and you've got to start over without him or any physical memories of him.

DO'S AND DON'TS OF ENDING LOVE

Do have the decency to tell him that it's over.
Don't give him the silent treatment and hope he'll get the message.
Don't write good-bye on the mirror in lipstick and think it's over.
Don't keep him on hold while you're trying to find a replacement.
Do give him equal time to express his feelings.
Don't pacify him by alluding to the possibility of getting back together.
Do be warm and friendly on the telephone.
Don't tease him when you know that you don't want him.
Don't suggest pairing him up with a friend.
Do invite him to a friend's party that you can't go to. This will allow him a chance to meet new people.
Don't throw up other prospects that you have in his face.
Don't continue to see him if you don't want him romantically.
Don't confront him if you see him with another woman.
Don't try to show up at the same place he is with another guy on the way to break up with him.

HEALING AFTER BREAKING UP

Healing from a broken relationship can be quite devastating, but you'll heal faster if you chart the stages from grief to rage to acceptance. The good thing about breaking up is that you lose weight, the bad thing is you cry all the time. When a relationship ends you come out of the cataclysm in stages. These stages are well defined. (In a recent New York Times survey, it is usually the man who gets dumped.) No matter what the sex, people go through breakups in very similar ways.

Here's a nine step path that most psychologists agree with that leads to healing:

1. BARGAINING: With fate or God. You offer something to c change in you to be a better person, let your hair grow out, lose weight or give up smoking if he'll come back to you.

2. GRIEVING: Tightness of the chest, difficulty breathing, emotional numbness, feeling desperate and abandoned.

3. PAIN: Anguish over the loss, a feeling of being deprived.

4. FEAR: Night terrors and sweats; you feel that you will be alone forever.

5. SADNESS: Deep sorrow that your life has led you to this point. You continue to say that your love affair could have worked or it almost worked.

6. ANGER: Rage that you were not valued by your lover. Rage at the other woman. Rage about the circumstances that brought the breakup on.

7. DEPRESSION: Moping, feelings that you can't make the effort anymore, can't go through the trouble to date, can't make small talk with men.

8. ACCEPTANCE: The beginning of wellness. You began to that you can and will survive without him. You appreciate what you had in the affair and understand that it's over.

9. HOPE AND REBUILDING: You begin to take better care of yourself. You start to have a good time when you're on a date. You are eager to meet new people.

These stages are as predictable as the obstacles to happiness in a fairy tale, and as, in such tales, the going is far from easy. There are three tough places where women I spoke with had the most trouble were: grieving, anger and acceptance.

Fantasies of happiness can sometimes overtake women. Making love and making dinner puts them on a natural high. In their words, the idea of keeping house is a turn on to them, so they see this man in their lives as the ultimate of satisfaction.Communication is difficult for women who men have completely cut off.They therefore remain in the grieving stage. Grief doesn't care who it picks on, and it can also hurt the woman who did the leaving. Many people think that it's easier to leave than to be left.

If you find it difficult or too painful to get over a lover sometimes seeking professional help is best. If you find it impossible to reach out to your loved ones, then going for help is essential. If you're dysfunctional on your job or you're having trouble eating or sleeping then you must get counseling and therapy. A physiological imbalance can be produced by deep internal reactions toward loss. Many women don't realize the shape that they're in. That's why it's so important to know when you're past the normal stage of grief reaction so that help can be found. Accepting the end of an affair helps women to understand the part that they played in the beginning as well as the ending of it. Even the breakup may not have been their choice they did, however accept and choose the man. Sometimes they may be less interested or even withdrawn in the affair Women who are in these types of affairs tend to ignore the signs of pure rejection by making excuses for their man's lack of interest. When a woman makes her man her whole world or she becomes obsessed with him, she is opening herself up to heartbreak and anguish.

A breakup has a way of revealing emotional baggage to you. Start letting yourself in on your emotions and find out what you are subjecting yourself to and then you can start to change your life. No matter how the style of loving changes, no matter how rough it appears or how heavy the load you appear to be carrying the road to recovery after a breakup is the fact that you took another chance on love. Even though wounded, you will heal. That's the positive news throughout this.

TM

Chapter 35

YOUR BEDROOM EXCITEMENT

What it takes for women to add excitement to their bedrooms is the focus of this chapter. Breasts and buttocks are not the keys to being excited in bed. You've got to possess the erotic qualities that drive men crazy in bed. Many a woman thinks it's their face, smile or even their bubbling sense of humor. But it's much more than any of these outward qualities. It's an extra ingredient that women possess that they can't quite explain.

Women who possess this ingredient can have men risk their careers, marriages and financial statements. Any woman who wants to be the woman who can drive men to ecstasy can become the mistress (or the wife who acts like the mistress), by developing a new mental attitude. Details on possessing qualities that will raise your level of love-making are covered in this chapter. You will be considered a perfect lover by your mate after this erotic makeover.

The sexual techniques, exercises, diet, psychology and understanding will add to the sex life you already possess. It will develop into an event of more erotic stimulation with pulsating earthshaking and successful adventures of love.

My experiences are purely personal and simply editorial. I have served on no dynamic sex committees or leading sex magazines, but I have served at some point and time on top of my lover. My experiences have also taught me to chart my erogenous zones and document my personal experiences. I have had conferences with strangers, friends, moms, coworkers, dads and psychologists.

Understand that sex is not a manipulative adventure, but it is a way to release tension and express love. Erotic women love men, sex and sensuality. Women should not be afraid to enjoy the pleasures that are brought in their bedrooms. Being able to give your man pleasures after you've read this chapter will make him love you even more.

Many women enter into sex without knowledge of where the penis is supposed to actually penetrate. My goal is to help mature, capable women fulfill their personal needs first, then to promote themselves into fulfilling their man's sexual needs.

Being unaware of what to do when faced with real life sexual encounters that are positive, healthy and wanted have been the dilemmas of many women. To add confidence to your bedroom excitementI will show you how to:
.Use bedroom tactics that work.
.Help him keep an erection.
.Please him orally.
.Accept your sexuality in a positive way.
.Turn a man on and keep a man turned on in bed, as well as out of bed.
.Communicate with him before going to bed with him
.Know what you're supposed to know.
.Increase female independence.

Potential sexual pleasures are within the reach of women and have a right to enjoy these unleased pleasures. You can train yourself to be a perfect lover. Erotic pleasures belong to you. With the knowledge and training you can be far from a slave to men.

To become more exciting in bed, you must cater to your man's fantasies. In achieving erotic pleasures a woman must do three things:

1. She must understand her own erotic potential and how to exploit it in a positive way with her lover.
2. She will know what her man wants most from her in bed and how to give it to him.
3. She will know how to go about getting and keeping the man she wants.

These three points are important, but the last point is the most important because not every woman has a man readily waiting in her bed. In fact, finding an exciting bed partner you want can be the most difficult part of the whole sexual exercise. Nothing is worse than being caught in a sexual relationship that has no spark. Exciting sex isn't something that we inherit. Training and counseling are essential even though it is physically and psychologically complex and in many cases affects our entire being. Every woman needs training that will equip her with the information to satisfy her lover, and will also give her the necessary means and understanding to use in a positive way.

Here are some suggested excitement chores that can help you learn to pay closer attention to your relationship. Some of them sound like simple housework, but each task can involve him more deeply as you add sexual excitement to your bedroom

1. Plan regular activities that involve you and him. It might be sexual or non sexual, anything that creates exciting rituals for the both of you.
2. Rent a romantic movie and then try to top the love scenes.
3. Plan your next vacation together and make sure it's a romantic get-away instead of visiting relatives.
4. Organize and plan dinners for two that are romantic and alluring. You should not invite the kids on these.
5. Keep track of social events and plan to spend happy times together.

BEDROOM MANNERS

I have a check list that covers the essentials. Some important things that women should remember about bedtime manners are:
*the owner of the bed delegates who will sleep on which side.
*try to wear something sexy to bed at least three hundred times in a year.
*provide toiletries for your partner such as towels, toothbrush.
*show him where the light switches are before retiring.
*don't make unnecessary noises while he's asleep.
*don't leave your bedtime gear at his place unless he asks.
*never take for granted that he'll be back the next week.
*Bring extra underwear if you sleep over, putting on the same
*underwear isn't very sexy after sex.
*Don't have excessive toiletries lying about, he'll think that your area is a heavily traffic area.
Moving your personal items in without notice is very inconsiderate.

If he wants to snuggle and you don't, COMPROMISE and do a little of both. If he snores, don't get angry, move to another location, but leave a little sexy note telling him where you are. End it with "Send Ransom."

BEDROOM MYTHS

There are many bedroom myths that circulate about the bedroom area. These sexual myths are no more realistically achievable than any others. The myths stop here.

#1. SEX DRAINS YOUR ENERGY
On the contrary, an energized love session can actually revitalize you. Some female athletes feel that their timing is much better when they have had good sex.

#2. TO LOOSEN UP OR RELIEVE TENSION, HAVE SEX
You would actually benefit more by having sex. It aids in normal fatigue that comes from hectic schedules. So go ahead and treat yourself to good, relaxing sex.

#3. HAVING SEX MORE, MAKES YOU WANT MORE
This is absolutely true. It's a life cycle. Even though studies are being made on this subject, one thing is for sure...hormones released with sexual activity increase sexual desire. Sex causes women to feel energized, restful, and sometimes slightly intoxicated, therefore creating a desire to have more sex.

#4. SEMEN IMPROVES YOUR COMPLEXION
According to Dr. John Ramono, vitamins need a co-factor to be absorbed through the intestine and cannot be absorbed through the skin. Therefore semen does not nourish the skin or prevent wrinkles as some people think. Semen is high in fructose, a form of sugar therefore as a topical skin treatment it would be unhealthy.

#5. SEX IS THE BEST WAY TO LOSE WEIGHT
This is true if you skip meals and make love every twelve hours. If not, forget it. No one has been able to give accurate counts on calories burned during love-making. The most popular estimates are:

> **foreplay=100 calories an hour**
> **intercourse=100 calories an hour**
> **orgasm=400 calories an hour**

Orgasm may sound like a dream come true to dieters, but most orgasms last only three to fifteen seconds. That's 1.6 calories at most per seismic event. The grand total is 201.6 calories for two hours and fifteen seconds.

#6. THE BEST LOVERS ARE PHYSICALLY FIT

Being physically fit helps natural functions to work better, but it does not determine the worst or the best in a woman. Some women feel that being in shape helps them to make love better. Physically fit bodies in the bedroom are gaining popular attention. Women out of shape tend to tire faster. Women who are in shape experience more powerful orgasms along with more forceful pelvic contractions. Being physically fit may not cure sex problems, but it will definitely elevate the mood.

#7. FLAT CHESTED WOMEN HAVE STRONG SEX DRIVES

Some do, some don't. Breast size has absolutely nothing to do with a woman's sex drive. Some women are stimulated by breast play, and to them the breast is extremely erotic. This doesn't matter whether breasts are big or small.

#8. BIRTH CONTROL PILLS INCREASE SEX DRIVE

Some women are more relaxed once they began taking the pill. They feel freer to let go and really enjoy sex.

#9. MASTURBATION CAUSES BLINDNESS

Masturbation is natural, healthy and in some cases therapeutic to preorgasmic women. Masters estimates that ninety percent of all men and eighty-five percent of all women in the civilized world masturbate. Modern sexologists assure us that although self-manipulation is not responsible for creating heaven and earth, it never hurt anyone either.

#10. EVERY ORGASM FEELS THE SAME

Orgasms come in a variety of feelings, from mild to industrial strength. The intensity of the orgasms can depend on various things such as time of day, mood, time of month. Orgasm myths can cause unnecessary worry for men and women. Women sometimes feel quiet orgasms that are sometimes just as pleasurable, says sex therapist Betti Krukofsky. A man likes to see women climax noisily so that he can enjoy his macho pride. If she's quiet he feels that he's failed.

#11. WOMEN DON'T NEED TO ALWAYS CLIMAX DURING SEX

If a women doesn't climax, the blood that fills the labia takes a while to dissipate and women may be left with an uncomfortable throbbing and bloated feeling. Women don't need to have an orgasm, but she feels much better when she does.

#12. MARRIED COUPLES HAVE SEX AT LEAST TWO OR THREE TIMES A WEEK

Couples in their twenties tend to have sex every day; thirty-to-forty years-olds have intercourse between two and three times a week; forty-to-fifty-years-old once a week; and sixty plus less than once a week. A couple can have sex twenty times a week, once a week or only on holidays. The problem exists if one partner wants sex more than the other.

#13. MARIJUANA IMPROVES SEX DRIVE

Smoking marijuana will not make your beloved more attractive to you, cure sexual hang ups or make him more imaginative in bed. Marijuana might put you in the mood and it might heighten your pleasure. Marijuana smokers tend to feel that their orgasms are more intense, but what is really happening is that her heart rate is speeding up to 240 beats each minute. This drug also induces an obsessive state of mind. Getting high distorts your perception of time, making you think sex is lasting much longer than it really is.

#14. SEX LENGTHENS LIFE

Aging does not mean the end of love-making, but information abounds on sex and the older man. His erection is not as rigid and more direct stimulation is required to attain an erection. Frequency of love-making is not linked to longevity.   Sex does make you want to live longer says William Masters.

™

Chapter 36

THINGS WOMEN FEAR IN BED

Fear blocks pleasure. If you are focusing more on your personal faults when you should be focusing on love-making you may be cheating yourself of one of life's greatest pleasures. Emotions are complicated and so is the list of anxieties that are taken to the bedroom. Most women are ashamed of their sexual fears, so they try to hide them from the men in their lives. Anxiety and secrecy reinforce one another. Embarrassment is certainly the key to the number one female question.

Body image:

Insecurity about a woman's body is a cover for a deeper sense of sexual shame, a fear that there is something unattractive about her body whether it be odor or genitals. Work to challenge old beliefs so that you can enjoy full sexual pleasure as an adult. Exploring your own feelings can release old baggage that you might be carrying around. Self-consciousness about the body is only one item in the catalog of common sexual fears.

Loss of erection:

When he suddenly begins to lose his erection during the heat of passion, most women blame themselves. The fact is, women are left in the cold on the subject because men just don't want to talk about their impotence. They are too fearful or embarrassed from the end results. Most women consider a man's inability or inability to have an erection is a direct measure of her desirability. Women are known to take the responsibility for the success of maintaining relationships. When men are having problems, women are expected to automatically fix the problem.

Asking questions instead of giving up on love can end many unexplained fears in a relationship that's gone cold. Sexual communication can calm, reduce and sometimes diminish fears about a man's sexual performance. People freeze up on conversations that they most need to talk about. Communications hold the key to reducing sexual problems.

Pregnancy:

Even intelligent and mature women take chances, says gynecologists. Women who may not be able to become pregnant when they want to is a new fear that is popping up. Women in this bracket try to get pregnant just to prove to themselves that they can conceive. If a woman in the "want to group" doesn't get pregnant without protection, then she begins to second guess her ability to conceive. This source of tension, and wondering creates questions of "Have I waited too long?" or "Can I afford to wait any longer?"

Taking chances without protection loads love-making with anxieties. It's much wiser to work out ambivalence about pregnancy by thinking or talking things over instead of scaring yourself each month by taking unnecessary chances with your body.

Oral sex:

Many women fear that they don't know what they are doing when it comes to oral sex. They think that they may bite their lovers penis or that they may gag. Some women are afraid to receive oral sex because they are ashamed of their genitals and can't believe a man would enjoy kissing or licking them. There is a tremendous amount of guilt and shame attached to oral sex. Even though many men are eager to perform it, many women are still quite ashamed to have it done for them. If you are ashamed to have it done for you tell him so.

Remember that he probably would not volunteer to do it if he didn't get pleasure from doing it.

<u>Growing older:</u>

Many women worry about losing their sex appeal as they began to enter their thirties. From the tiny lines in her face, to the fact that her body tone is becoming more difficult to keep, causes a woman to worry. Sex is usually a very important part of a woman. The claim that women don't reach their sexual peaks until their forties is hard to believe. Experts say that it's true and studies confirm that women enjoy sex more as they gain experience and control in their lives. Traditional attitudes have caused women to think less of their sexual appetites. Our mothers lived restricted sex lives and they looked much older at our age now than we do. Fear of expressing sexual wants and desires have helped to age our parents because of all the stipulations and anxieties on sexual freedoms. Taking on younger lovers used to be condemned, but now it's a natural part of a sexually aggressive and free women. The major fears women have had are due to rules set by men on what women should and can be sexually. The truth is, many men just can't keep pace sexually with women.

Let things happen naturally

Chapter 37

SIGNS OF A SEXUAL DUD

If a woman pays attention to the cues, she'll possibly be able to spot a sexual dud before she wastes her time. Sexual duds give off very clear signals that women can read very easily. These men are narsistic and self-centered from the very beginning. Many women ignore the obvious signs because he either makes her feel like he's MR. RIGHT or he brags on his sexual abilities or conquests. Some of the usual signs to watch for are:

~Sexual duds ignore the fact that they are duds because they are so busy trying to prove themselves to a woman that they ignore their inabilities.

~He builds himself up verbally to compensate for his lack of sexual prowness.

~He cannot be measured in inches and he is often over-bearing and demanding.

~He will always order dinners for the both of you, he won't let you drive your car and he's obviously accustomed to controlling his lovers.

~His bedroom manners will reflect his personality so watch for tacky signs.

~Men who are driven to perform athletically will usually have less left for love-making.

~Some men put so much energy into sports that they try to compensate for their poor performance in sex.

SEXUALLY DULL TYPES:

1. HE'S TOO SERIOUS.
He's perfect in his eyesight, but the world and all else in it is not. He verbally curses out automobile drivers. He's critical of restaurants food and your taste. This guy will not cuddle or give affection.

2. YOU'RE JUST MY TYPE.
If he reminds you that you're just his type... Watch Out. The woman he's with is the measure of being a man. Women are sexual objects in his eyes.

3. THE UNSAFE MAN.
He doesn't talk about safe sex and is irresponsible to contraception. Only thinks of his fulfillment.

4. THE UNFULFILLED MAN.
He has low self-esteem and constantly talks of his bad luck. He feels powerless and useless. He expects everything to be a let down and he's probably right.

Chapter 38

PROPS AND SUPPLIES

SEXUAL HOPE CHESTS

Women should have hope chests filled with the necessary props and supplies that will help in adding variety to their sensuous love-making. Most of these items are probably accessible right in your home. These ideas were given to me by women I interviewed throughout my research. Feel free to vary as needed to add or deplete the spice. Listed here are props and supplies that every woman should have on hand as an alternate to ordinary sex.

1. **Flavored cough drops** can be used as a stimulator toward sex. Suck on the cough drop a few minutes or so before sex. During oral sex the female will blow on the penis lightly as she sucks on it. Your hot tongue and the moisture from your mouth along with the menthol fresh coolness from the cough drop will create a cool sensation to his penis. This will help the male to keep a very nice and stiff erection. Continue this thrill until he begs for mercy. Remember to vary your moves.

2. **Whipped cream** can be used on all of your man's erogenous zones. Some favorite places are: nipples, stomach navel, neck ears, toes, buttocks, penis, fingers and other hot spots that you can think of. Be careful not to get it inside the ears. This simple seduction is very inviting because you have to eat the whipped cream from your lovers body. Use slow, seductive licks to eat it off. Alternate your tongue motions by slipping and sliding your tongue in continuous lavishing licks. This one will send chills throughout your lover's entire body and his excitement will in turn arouse you.

3. **Flavored lip gloss** can be used on both sets of a woman lips. Buy two different flavors to distinguish which will be used on each pair of lips. Every woman can't use this seductive tip because of the sensitivity of her skin. To apply this lip gloss method of seduction, spread your lips and roll on the lip gloss. The roll on lip gloss is best for this method because it glides right onto your vaginal lips. This is not to alter the taste or smell, but to add to it.

4. **Assorted lingerie** is nice to wear on almost any occasion. Men won't always admit the fact that a woman in beautiful lingerie is a turn on, but watch the sparks fly when you approach him or unveil your body dressed in this beautiful attire. Make sure your bras and panties match, are clean and are sexy when you're going to be with your lover. It adds to the sensuality of the mood.

5. **Sun glasses** of assorted frames and styles are glamorous when worn correctly. When wearing casual wear, wear your favorite casual sun glasses. When wearing your most glamorous attire wear a pair of shades that fits the occasion. Every woman should have more than one pair of sun glasses to accommodate her wardrobe.

6. **Men suits** are hot on a sexy and sensuous woman. A woman can wear a man's suit and add flair that invites the masculine side of the man to chill out. Women in sensuous suits turn men on in more ways than one. Accompany the suit with a low cut blouse or no blouse at all. Accessorize with small delicate jewelry.

7. **Finger nail polish** adds allure and beauty to a woman's nails. Adding color to the nails sends out beautiful messages to a man whether he's your man or not. I personally know men who won't date a woman unless she is well manicured.

8. Fruits like bananas, strawberries, cherries, pineapple chunks are nice as an additive to oral sex. If you'd like to have your sex and eat it to try pieces of fruit as a delight. You can also place pieces of assorted fruit onto your lover's body and eat it off.

9. Long coats are nice when you want to visit your man in nothing but your underwear. Think of these coats as long dresses, and you'll be able to pull it off. Most women began to play mind games with themselves because they won't allow themselves to be free of stigmas. Be sensuous and romantic for your man, and you'll go far with his heart this way. Wear the coat with nice lingerie or a teddy in his favorite color.

10. Aprons greet him at the door in nothing but an apron tied around your sensuous waist.

11. Toiletries are great for your lover when he sleeps over and has left his toiletries at his home. Having a few items of his favorite brands accessible is being considerate and in tune to his needs. Keep a little basket under your counter for him with toothpaste, colognes, shaver or razor, comb, brush, after shave. Anything that you think your man might need to make his stay a little more comfortable makes him feel more connected.

12. Oils and lotions are enriching to his skin when they're readily available for a nice massage before or after sex. Men love a sensuous massage at any time.

13. Popsicles are a terrific turn on for your lover as he watches you penetrate, lick and penetrate again. Use this as a means of erotic foreplay. It works wonders. Assorted popsicles are best.

14. Chilled wine or champagne is stimulating when poured over his body and licked off, or used for dipping pleasure. Dip his penis into a filled glass of champagne and then lick it off to his delight. He'll get goose bumps and you'll get turned on as you turn him on. Watch his beef rise to new heights.

15. Mr. Good-Bars are given as a gesture to tell him he's good. The best time to send him a giant Mr. Good Bar is the day after sex. Personally deliver it to him wrapped in gift paper or in a gift box, or have it delivered to him by a delivery company. He'll be ringing your phone off the hook after he receives this

this delightful message. You don't have to write a note or send a card with it unless you want because the candy bar will say it all.

16. Fresh Condoms are a necessity for every sexually active woman and man. Having fresh condoms is not only smart, but also wise. Don't expect your lover to provide this protection for you. A smart sensuously mature women will be responsible for her own sexual protection. Condoms also have a life span. Make sure that your condoms are not old and outdated. This has bearing on the effectiveness of your protection. Remember to use jelly with your condoms , because twice the protection is just as nice.

17. Breath mints are a handy necessity for any woman who kissing and talking to someone closely.

18. Candles are romantic, soothing and alluring whether alone or with your lover. When alone, candles add a special and personal atmosphere that helps you to enjoy time with yourself. They lull you to moments of subtle interludes. When with your lover, watch television by candlelight, take baths by candlelight or just sit in the dark and talk by candlelight. Who can resist being romantic when the setting is so mellow.

19. Other lights and illuminations are nice peeking in from other rooms. Dimly lit or colored light bulbs add romantic overtures also. They decrease electric bills if you're living on a budget. Enjoy the magic of subtle lighting and enjoy your atmosphere.

20. Incense, potpourri or other aromas set the mood and enhance the atmosphere. The aroma creates waves of feelings and erotic moods. It's all in your thought process, so think sexy thoughts.

21. Tape measures come in handy when playing measurement games with your lover. If he's confident in his penis size, its fun to measure his length and width of his penis. Don't use this as a ridicule tool later on. This is only used to get a rise out of his penis and your temperature.

22. Handkerchiefs squirted with a little perfume are nice to carry in your purse or pocket. The cloth keeps the aroma of a beautiful scent on your body.

23. <u>Costumes</u> are a nice turn on for men. Keep him at home by changing your look for his pleasure. Men like the idea of having more than one woman. So why don't you be that multiple person. Change your hair, clothes and any other features from time to time to add spice to an otherwise routine relationship. Dress up to look like his favorite starlet or sex goddess, or create your own look of sexiness for him. He'll be pleasantly surprised at your efforts to please him.

24. <u>Love notes</u> are designed just for him. Leave them everywhere he'll be. Keep them simple and personalized. Be sure to say little things in your notes that will push his erotic buttons, something that only you and he could relate to. A code or key word that the two of you use will work wonders.

25. <u>Create your own scenes</u> by decorating your home or apartment for a romantic trip to your favorite vacation place. If your favorite place is Rome, do as the Romans do and invent your pleasures from the scenery to the food you eat. Create a wonderful and romantic atmosphere of love for two. Stop by a travel agency and pick up brochures and travel information to your favorite vacation spot. Remember the little things like the foods, the pleasures and the souvenirs that are found at your selected place of escape. Your lover will be surprised as well as enchanted with your thoughtfulness. The key is to escape entirely by playing the role completely.

26. <u>Sweet additives</u> like honey, sugar, chocolate, and other delights can add tasty pleasures to your appetite. Try a few and see which ones suit your taste.

27. <u>Balloons or flowers</u> are fantastic when trying to make up or add cheer to your lovers day. For no reason at all send balloons or flowers and a message to let him know that you are thinking of him. He'll be a little shy about it at first, but the idea of it all will send happiness and sheer delights to his brain.

28. <u>Picnics</u> don't have to be in the park. Why not have one for two in your living room, your back yard, on a patio or even in your bedroom. Fireplace picnics are a favorite also. Simply prepare a picnic basket with your favorite wine and foods; select a place to have it and indulge in the fun of it all. Have you ever had a nude picnic? Try it and don't forget to add your own spice to it.

29. Pearls are nice when worn alone. Greet him at the door in a single strand of pearls. Make sure he's the only one who gets a glimpse of you. If he can guess how many pearls are on the strand, he'll be able to choose his sexual pleasure for the day.

30. Read to him it is sensuous if he can sit still long enough to listen. Find your copy of Will The Real Women Please Stand Up and read a chapter or two that's sure to turn him on. If he gets turned on before you finish, don't worry you can always start over when you need to excite him again.

31. Silk scarves should touch him lightly all over his naked body. You can also use silk scarves as aprons before stripping in front of him to music.

TM

Chapter 39

CONTRACEPTIVES

The Pill, the Condom, the Diaphragm, the Sponge, Norplant, and Sterilization. These are options available for birth control today. Women would like more information instead of new choices. Birth control is one of the major issues facing women in the nineties.

As fears of sexually transmitted diseases and pregnancies, including STD's and HIV which causes AIDS monopolize our thoughts, intelligent contraceptive selection is more important than ever before. Making that choice can be confusing no matter how sexually experienced a woman is. Here is IMPORTANT information on what you need to know about contraceptives: Before trying any contraceptives, be sure to check with your doctor for the best method for you.

THE PILL:

Effectiveness: 94 to 97 percent
Used by: 10.8 million American women which is 31% of contraceptive users.

Cost: About $250.00 a year

The pill is the second most popular choice of birth control (after sterilization) in this country, and the most often used by women aged fifteen to forty four. It offers control over fertility has ease of use and is one of the most worry free methods around. Pill users can expect regular periods with less bleeding, cramping and pre-menstrual comfort. Risks are both ectopic pregnancy and pelvic inflammatory disease (PID), a potential life threatening condition. The pill use may reduce incidence of anemia, acne and rheumatoid arthritis.

Protection against ovarian and endometrial cancers is probably the pill's biggest advantage. Women who have used this method at any time during their lives have one-fifth the chance of developing either of these diseases as do women who haven't. Cancer risk has sometimes decreased as length of pill use increases.

There are several disadvantages to oral-contraceptive use, including such hormone related side effects as an altered menstrual cycle, headaches, nausea, weight change and mood swings. The pill is not recommended for women over thirty-five who smoke or for those with cardio-vascular irregularities.

Pill users who decide they want to become pregnant are advised to switch to another form of birth control several months before trying to conceive.

THE CONDOM

Effectiveness: 86 to 90 percent when used alone; 98 percent when combined with a spermicide.
Used by: 5.2 million American women (15 percent of contraceptive users)
Cost: Approximately .50 cents per condom

The condoms main advantage, especially in recent years, is that it is the most effective of all contraceptives in preventing the spread of STD, and the only one known to impede the transmission of the AIDS virus. Condoms are also inexpensive and available without a prescription. Over half of all condoms are purchased by women.

Latex (rubber) condoms are the only kind that should be used if protection against STD's is a concern. (The more-porous lambskin types prevent pregnancy only.) Latex condoms differ in effectiveness: some are more prone to breakage and slippage than others. A wise choice is condoms lubricated with the spermicide nonoxynol-9. But no matter what type you use always use a spermicide as a part of the procedure.

On the down side, some couples claim that condoms reduce spontaneity and sensation. Some women even report allergic reactions to latex.

THE DIAPHRAGM

Effectiveness: 98 percent
Used by: Two million American women (6 percent of con-
traceptive users)
Cost: $120.00 to $180.00 per year

Many women appreciate that the diaphragm is unobtrusive and, if inserted beforehand (up to six hours), does not affect spontaneity. Like other barrier methods, the diaphragm which must be used with spermicidal jelly or cream. It provides some protection against STD's and PID.

Diaphragm use does, however, have a drawback, namely, an increased risk of urinary-tract and bladder infections. Furthermore, spermicide must be reapplied each time you have sex, and allergic reactions to the spermicide or to the device itself are possible.

The diaphragm must be fitted by your doctor, and refitting may be required after weight loss or gain, child birth, or pelvic surgery. Users should also be aware that the diaphragm is more likely to be dislodged in the female-on-top position.

THE SPONGE

Effectiveness: 72 to 82 percent
Used by: 244,000 American women (0.7 percent of
contraceptive users)
Cost: Approximately $1.50 per sponge

A relatively new method, the contraceptive sponge (a round piece of polyurthane about two inches in diameter that is treated with the spermicide nonoxynol-9) can be used by women who can wear tampons. It offers twenty-four hour protection, meaning there's no interruption in spontaneity. Users are offered some protection from STD's.

The sponge should not be used during menstruation, nor should it be used by women who have had toxic-shock syndrome. Some allergic reactions are possible. Be sure to consult your physician before use.

FOAMS, CREAMS, AND JELLIES

Effectiveness: 79 percent when used alone; up to 98 percent when used with a condom.

Used by: 209,000 American women (0.6 percent of contraceptive users)

Cost: About $1.50 per application

Use of spermicidal foams, creams or jellies offer some protection against STD's. Some products may not dissolve completely, however, increasing the risk of conception. Furthermore, all spermicides must be reapplied with each act of intercourse and users may experience more urinary-tract infections than non-users.

THE INTRAUTERINE DEVICE (IUD)

Effectiveness: 94 percent

Used by: 700,00 American women (2 percent of contraceptive users)

Cost: Approximately $90 for Progestasert, $300 for Copper T

Today's IUDs-progesterone-releasing Progestasert and copper-based Copper T-do not carry the same risks as their predecessor, the Dalkon Shield. Sold to more than 2.2 million women in the early seventies, the Shield has been blamed for pelvic infections resulting in infertility, devastating and prolonged pain, even death. The cause was thought to be a tail-string, used exclusively on the Shield, that drew bacteria from the vagina into the uterus.

Although Progestasert and Copper T are definite improvements over Dalkon, they're far from risk-free. Copper T users run twice the risk of pelvic infection as do women who use no contraception at all and may suffer excessive bleeding and cramping. Ectopic pregnancy and infertility are other possible consequences. Of the two, Progestasert, which must be replaced annually (Copper T can remain in place six years), is less likely to cause heavy menstrual flow and cramps, but its ectopic pregnancy rate is six to ten times higher than that of the Copper T.

THE CERVICAL CAP

Effectiveness: 87 to 98 percent
Used by: 40,000 American women (0.4 percent of contraceptive users)
Cost: $50.00- $150.00

The cervical cap is the least popular of all forms of birth control. A close relative of the diaphragm, it provides forty-eight hours of protection without spermicide reapplication. It also helps prevent STD's.

A pap smear and a prescription are needed to obtain the cervical cap, which is harder to insert and easier to dislodge than the diaphragm. As a result, the caps failure rate may run as high as twenty-five percent for women under the age of thirty who have sex at least four times a week.

NORPLANT

Effectiveness: 99.5 percent
Used by: 55,000 American women (in Food and Drug Administration testing only)
Cost: about $800.00, including doctor's fee, for up to five years of protection.

The first major new contraceptive method to be FDA-approved in nearly three decades, Norplant is a set of six-match-stick like progesterone filled tubes that are inserted under the skin of the upper arm. This simple surgical procedure under local anesthesia in a doctor's office. Once in place, Norplant remains effective for up to five years, unless the user chooses to have it removed. Fertility is then immediately restored.

Because this method is so new, a limited number of doctors are currently trained to insert Norplant. Disadvantages include side effects similar to, although less severe than, those of the Pill: altered menstrual cycle, headaches, weight change, nausea. Their severity tends to lessen, after six to nine months of use.

Norplant is also less effective in women who weigh more than 150 pounds, and those with certain medical conditions-heart problems, liver disease, diabetes, high cholesterol, high blood pressure, breast cancer, or a history of blood clots may not be good candidates for this method. Norplant is viewed as a long term alternative to permanent sterilization.

STERILIZATION

Effectiveness: Tubal Ligation, 99.6 percent; vasectomy, 99.8 percent

Used by: 9.8 million American women and 4.2 million American men (40 percent of contraceptive users)

Cost: $1,500.00 to $2,500 for tubal ligation; $ 350.00 to $750.00 vasectomy

Besides being the only permanent method of contraception, sterilization is sole nonbarrier method not tied to any long-term risks. Couples who choose sterilization must be absolutely certain they don't want any more children. As many as seventy percent of tubal ligations and fifty percent of vasectomies cannot be reversed.

Tubal ligation performed in a hospital under general anesthesia is considered major surgery but carries only slight risks of infection and other complications. No such risks exists for vasectomies, which are done under local anesthesia in a doctor's office. There has been an increase in the number of tubal ligations in recent years, which one study attributes to women opting for sterilization after having their IUD's removed.

Research is presently being conducted on a female vaccine that would produce antibodies against pregnancy. Three formulas are currently in development.

Get physically involved with your community

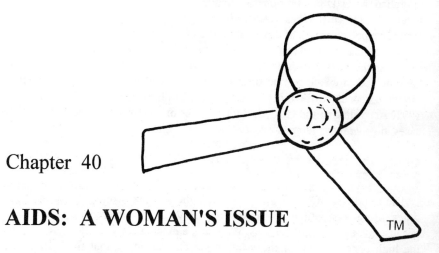

Chapter 40

AIDS: A WOMAN'S ISSUE

Until very recently, Aids studies have concentrated on the affects of HIV in men. Learning the truth is now becoming clearer as women are accepting the facts to protect themselves, because AIDS is a women's issue.

Dating several men; sleeping with them, and not paying attention to the disease is one of the major problems with women who contract the AIDS virus. Young women worry about getting pregnant, more than getting HIV.

Eleven years after it's debut as a "gay man's disease," the AIDS epidemic has acquired a new face-female. Approximately 28,000 women have been reported with AIDS and approximately 150,000 are likely to be affected with H.I.V., the virus that causes AIDS. Symptoms of life threatening AIDS don't develop until about five years after being in affected.

African Americans influence about half of all the cases and Hispanic women about one fifth. These numbers don't tell the complete story of this epidemic among women because it doesn't tell about the women who are infected with H.I.V. These women have certain symptoms that include cancer of the cervix, pelvic infections, vaginal yeast infections, pneumonia and tuberculosis. Women have died because of these diseases, but they have never been counted as victims of the deadly disease. Despite evidence that some of these diseases are more common and severe in women infected with H.I.V.; gynecological disorders or cancers were not listed as apart of AIDS-defining infections. Centers for Disease Control and Prevention (CDC) have been reluctant to add these conditions because they also infect women without H.I.V. The CDC upgraded its AIDS definition to include invasive cervical cancer and blood levels of CD4 cells. These cells help to fight infections and low blood levels increase a person's risks of developing diseases.

Women recognized as having AIDS has steadily risen, and will continue to rise over the next decade. New additions by the CDC to the AIDS definition have helped to create this boost in numbers of women with AIDS. The AIDS infection accounted for thirty-seven percent of all cases of AIDS in women in 1991. According to the CDC, and the number of heterosexually acquired AIDS cases in general has jumped twenty-five percent each year from 1989 to 1992.

SUSCEPTIBILITY OF AIDS IN WOMEN

The rapid rise of AIDS in women, and the fact that women are at least ten times more susceptible to contracting HIV during intercourse than men, because of several noted reasons. Women are much more vulnerable because of the high concentration of the virus in semen than in vaginal fluid. It is also possible for the virus of the infected semen to slip easily into a woman's body by way of vaginal sores from other sexually transmitted diseases (STD's) or tiny cuts and tears found in the vagina or labia.

AIDS research prevention and treatment strategies for women have been slowed by the government. Some women health advocates have used this fact as part of the blame for the current women's AIDS epidemic in this country. The false accusations that women who fostered the virus were prostitutes, promiscuous, or either I.V. drug users led the government to disregard any other women as being in the HIV path. The alarm was not sounded soon enough and now more women have become at risk for getting AIDS. Any of us can get AIDS. You do not have to sleep with several men to get AIDS, noted Charles C.J. Carpenter, M.D., professor of medicine at Brown University. Many women with AIDS who acquire it heterosexually were seeing only one man when they contacted the HIV virus. Many of these women had sexual relationships with men who didn't even know that they had the virus. Many men who carry the virus keep it to themselves while continuing to have intercourse with women or wives without using condoms.

YOU MUST PROTECT YOURSELF

There are many things that you as a women can do to protect yourself. The standard AIDS- prevention questions are:

1. Ask your partner if he's had a positive AIDS test.
2. Ask him if he's had sex with multiple partners recently or other men.
3. Ask him if he's used intravenous drugs.
4. Ask him if he's engaged in sexual practices where the skin was broken during sex.
5. Ask him if he's had unprotected sex.
6. Ask him if he's had a blood transfusion.

 * If he answers yes to any of these questions, he's at risk of having the AIDS virus. There is no guarantee that a man will answer truthfully to the listed questions. He may not know that he has slept with an infected person, or he may not want you to know that he is carrying the virus. In addition to this fact, a person infected with the virus results can take up to six months to show up on a test. It is positively essential to practice safe sex unless you are certain that he is faithful, or he has been tested for the virus and retested after every six months.

Practicing safe sex is sometimes difficult, but there are ways to protect yourself. Using the latex male condom is the only weapon available at this time, besides abstinence. Studies have shown that the use of condoms have been highly effective at preventing the spread of H.I.V. Many men refuse to use condoms and women sometimes submit to their lover's requests by making love without condom use. Here are a few sensuous ways to effectively slip a condom on your lover's penis.

1. Be as erotic as possible about using condoms.
2. Offer to put it on for him, and as you put it on him massage his penis sensuously.   There's no need to be afraid to do it because it's for your safety also.
3. Be sure to add lubricants that are water based such as K-Y Jelly. Vaseline corrodes condoms, so don't use it.
4. Try using colorful or textured condoms to add variety.
5. Use the condom as the avenue to turn him on.
6. Have healthy love play by discussing condoms with your lover or even members of your family. Surprisingly, many women lack interest in their

own health priority. This same group of women tend to take care of everyone in the family, but lack taking care of themselves.

WOMEN'S INFORMATION LINE

Trying not to be reckless with your body as well as your sexuality can cause uncertainty and uneasiness. From **women's issues to AIDS to sexual matters to health issues** unique to women just like you... Call The Women's Information Line... You'll Feel Better Knowing.

To order this book for friends or family: Call toll free:

Will The Real Women Please Stand Up
        (1-800-269-6228)

APPENDICES

FOR WOMEN WHO READ THIS BOOK

This questionnaire is anonymous, so you don't have to sign it. Every question does not need to be answered. Answer only the questions that you are interested in. You don't even have to complete it. Just reply as you wish to. You may not choose to answer any of the questions. You may want to create your own. Just send it in. Please mail questions, answers and comments to:

Knowledge Concepts Educational Services
c /o Ella Jones Patterson
P.O. Box 973
Cedar Hill, Texas 75104

1. Have you had the opportunity to read Will The Real Women Please Stand Up? Which sections, chapters or issues do you agree with? Disagree?
2. Which part of this book is the most important to you? Least important? Most emotional?
3. Has your sensuality changed since you read this book? In what way?
4. Is orgasm easier for you since reading this book?
5. Are orgasms important to you or do you enjoy sex just as much without orgasms?
6. When do you have orgasms? During intercourse? Masturbation? Clitoral stimulation? Other sexual activities? How often?
7. Do you have orgasms during intercourse? Never? Sometimes? Rarely?
8. Remembering your most favorite orgasm, give a description of how your body is stimulated to orgasm.
9. Please give ways that you and your partner practice direct stimulation.
10. What kind of stimulation of the clitoral area do you prefer? Do you prefer hard, medium, or soft massage? Do you like continuous movement? Do you like your positions varied?
11. Do you like intercourse? Physically? Psychologically ? Do you have any physical discomfort?

12. Do you enjoy masturbation? Physically? Psychologically? Is it more intense with or without a partner?
13. Do you enjoy rectal contact? What kind? Do you enjoy penetration? How often do you do it?
14. What do you think about during sex? Do you have fantasies? What about?
15. Do you look ugly or beautiful during orgasms?
16. Do you think that most men are uninformed about what pleases women?
17. Do you like objects in bed with you? Do you like to use objects in love-making?
18. Do you have intercourse during your period? Do you have oral sex during your period?
19. What are your best sex experiences?
20. How long do your sexual encounters last?
21. Do you have sex with the people you want to have sex with? Do you usually initiate the sex or the sexual advances?
22. Do you enjoy touching? Whom do you touch-men, women, friends, relatives, children, yourself, animals, pets?
23. Do you feel politically inclined to have sex?
24. Do you masturbate with your partner during sex? During general caressing? Was it difficult to do the first time that you did it? How did you feel about it?
25. Please add anything you would like to say that was not mentioned in this questionnaire at the end of this questionnaire.
26. Have you discussed your sexual relationship with any other women? Have you discussed masturbation with them or not? What did she say? What did she think?
27. Do you like this questionnaire?
28. What else would you like to talk about or find out about sex?
29. Why did you answer this questionnaire?
30. Are you in love?
31. Are you happy?
32. What makes you happiest in life?
33. What sex is the person that you are closest to?
34. What is your biggest sexual problem?

35. What is your favorite way to spend time alone?
36. Does having children increase or decrease your sex drive?
37. How do you feel about pornography?
38. Have you ever had an affair or sex with a married man?
39. How often do you have sex with your partner? Would your relationship with your partner be in danger if sex decreased?
40. How often do you want or like to have sex?
41. Does sex with you lover change for the better? The worst? Does it become boring or more pleasurable?
42. Do certain conflicts in your relationship tend to last for years or over long periods of time? Have you found that the same problems keep cropping up even after you've talked about them or thought that they were worked out?
43. What do like most about your man? Least? What qualities do you admire most in your man? Dislike?
44. What do women tend to need most from men, if anything? Is there something you get from men that you can't get from women?
45. What effect does falling in love play in a man's life? Do you think that men take falling in love seriously?
46. Have you ever been financially dependent on a man? What problems if any, did it create? How did you feel about it? Did it ruin your relationship?
47. Have you ever been deeply hurt by a lover? How? What happened to hurt you? How soon did you get over it?
48. What emotional mood swings do you go through in your relationships?
49. Have you ever hated a man? Describe the man you hated the most. Why did you hate him? Did you remain angry for a long time? Did you tell your friends? How did they react?
50. Have you ever felt like you had to work to keep a man? Did you have fear of him leaving you? Losing his love? Did you ever feel that he would grow tired of you? Love you less?
51. Do you, or does he usually break up the relationship?
52. Do you ever feel that your sexual needs are unhealthy? Kinky? Dependent?

53. Do you feel that your love is too blind or too desperate? Do feel that your need for affection is excessive or overbearing?

54. Do you feel more secure when in love? Do you think that love is a problem for most women?

55. Are you afraid that you will make him feel tied down if you express your love to him?

56. Do you turn to men or women when in trouble?

57. What was the most important relationship with a women in your life?

58. Describe your closest female friend. What does she look like? How much time do you spend together? How do you act or feel after seeing her? What was your relationship like?

59. Is love between women different from love between men? Is this relationship healthy? Is it more emotional and sincere?

60. Have you ever fallen in love with another women? Would you like to fall in love with a woman?

61. Who is the person you have loved most in your life?

62. Who made you feel the most alive, the most you in your life? The most loved and cared for?

63. How do you define love? Is falling in love the thing that you work for in a relationship over a long period of time?

64. Was there anything that you would like to say and didn't?

THANK YOU

TM

INDEX

INDEX

INDEX

INDEX

SHOWER COLLECTIONS

You can delight the mother-to-be or the bridal couple and your guests with a collection of favorite recipes, memories and advice for the bride and groom with a Knowledge Concepts Shower Book or Cookbook.

By simply enclosing our collection form and following the step by step process, you can involve evryone in the fun of publishing a favorite book.

Our shower books or cookbooks feature a beautiful shower sentiment in soft colors on a personalized cover. Your book can feature not only recipes but also your guests' special greetings and memories of the couple.

Your party will live on for years with your guests being able to enjoy a collection of everyone's best recipes.

"Marriage is a promise to share on life together"

FAMILY COOKBOOKS

You can easily compile a unique Family Cookbook keepsake with Knowledge Concepts Publishing System. Imagine the value and memories to your children and grandchildren of having a collection of special recipes that were family favorites of past generations.

Your cookbook can be a distinctively personal keepsake with the addition of personal stories, anecdotes or children artwork.

Knowledge Concepts Publishing offers beautiful family cover selections or you can produce your own design to be personalized, bound and laminated on your books.

Family Cookbooks are a perfect family reunion project or a wonderful surprise gift for your family or friend on any special occassion. We guarantee everyone you share your cookbook with will be delighted with your recipe collection.

ORDER FORM

Telephone Orders: Call Toll Free 1-(800)-269-6228
Postal Orders: Make check or money order payable to:
Knowledge Concepts Educational Systems,
P.O. Box 973, Cedar Hill, Texas   75104

Please send the following books.

_____	1. *1000 Reasons To Think*	*$14.95*
_____	2. *Will The Real Women Please Stand Up*	*$14.95*
_____	3. *For Women Who Live Alone*	*$19.95*
_____	4. *Teenage Etiquette Guide*	*$10.95*
_____	5. *Basic Hygiene...Do It For Yourself*	*$ 9.95*
_____	6. *Easy Alternatives For Healthy Eating*	*$12.99*

se rush me copies of the following book(s). I have enclosed the price of each book plus
) per book for shipping and handling cost. I understand that if I am not completely
fied, I may return the book(s) within 10 days for a full refund. All books must be
emished to qualify for a full refund. Covers not torn, interior like new. If books are
iged in return process it is the buyers business to collect from the shipper. Please add my
e to your mailing lists to so that I may receive more information on any new books that you
written.

*ie:*_____

*ress:*_____

*:*_____

*e:*_____Zip:_____

tax: (per order)
se add 8.25% for books shipped to Texas addresses.

ing Fees:
Rate: $3.00 for the first book and $2.00 for each additional
. (Surface shipping may take three to four weeks)
ail Fees :$4.00 per book

ient Options:
k, Cashier's Check or Money order's please.
Amount Enclosed $_____

*Signature*_____

REUNION DIRECTORY

Allow Knowledge Concepts Publishing to ease the burden from your reunion committee by professionally producing a Knowledge Concepts Customized Directory for your group or reunion.

By including our collection form with your reunion invitation, we can help you compile a directory of your groups names, addresses, memories, and accomplisments.

You may add statistics, trivia, and news events to create a lasting momento of the event.

These projects often fund themselves by offering your participants advertising in your program. Save your efforts for planning and enjoying this event.

Custom Projects

Your group, office, or club will enjoy the team process of publishing a collection of best recipes, poems, or favorite short stories. You may wish to sell your book as a fund raiser or enjoy them as a personal keepsake.

Request for Publishing Information

lease send me a Publishing Planning Package for the following project

*   Family Cookbook
*   Baby Shower Collection
*   Bridal Shower Collection
*   Reunion Directory
*   Custom Project (Describe below)

_____

_____

_____

_____

_____

end Materials To:

Name_____

Address_____

City/State_____Zip_____

Home Phone(_____)_____
I tentatively plan to complete my project by the following date:

_____

ail To: Knowledge Concepts Publishing
P. O. Box 973
Cedar Hill, Texas   75104-0973
1-800-269-6228

Knowledge Concepts Publishing

To order additional copies of books by
Ella Jones Patterson
please contact
Knowledge Concepts Educational Systems at:

Knowledge Concepts Publishing
P.O. Box 973
Cedar Hill, Texas 75104-0973
1-800-269-6228

At Knowledge Concepts Publications, books are special. It's a place to
publish your family or group's memories, be it recipes, short stories
or poems. Our company is delighted to be able to offer
you professional publishing at an affordable price.

*Personal Publishing
*Cookbooks
*Short Stories
*Poems
*Reunion Directories